CULTURES OF THE WORLD
Tibet

Cavendish
Square

New York

Published in 2017 by Cavendish Square Publishing, LLC
243 5th Avenue, Suite 136, New York, NY 10016
Copyright © 2017 by Cavendish Square Publishing, LLC

Third Edition

This publication represents the opinions and views of the author based on his or her personal experience, knowledge, and research. The information in this book serves as a general guide only. The author and publisher have used their best efforts in preparing this book and disclaim liability rising directly or indirectly from the use and application of this book.
CPSIA Compliance Information: Batch #CW17CSQ
All websites were available and accurate when this book was sent to press.

Library of Congress Cataloging-in-Publication Data

Names: Levy, Patricia, 1951- author. | Bosco, Don, author. | Nevins, Debbie, author.
Title: Tibet / Patricia Levy, Don Bosco, and Debbie Nevins.
Description: 3rd edition. | New York : Cavendish Square Publishing, [2017] | Series: Cultures of the world |
Includes bibliographical references and index.
Identifiers: LCCN 2016034386 (print) | LCCN 2016034651 (ebook) | ISBN 9781502622136 (library bound) | ISBN 9781502622143 (E-book)
Subjects: LCSH: Tibet Autonomous Region (China)--Juvenile literature.
Classification: LCC DS786 .L456 2017 (print) | LCC DS786 (ebook) | DDC 951/.5--dc23
LC record available at https://lccn.loc.gov/2016034386

Writers: Patricia Levy and Don Bosco; Debbie Nevins, third edition
Editorial Director, third edition: David McNamara
Editor, third edition: Debbie Nevins
Associate Art Director, third edition: Amy Greenan
Designer, third edition: Jessica Nevins
Production Coordinator, third edition: Karol Szymczuk
Cover Picture Researcher: Angela Siegel
Picture Researcher, third edition: Jessica Nevins

PICTURE CREDITS

PRECEDING PAGE

Colorful prayer flags flutter in the breeze with the sacred Mount Kailash in the background.

Printed in the United States of America

CONTENTS

TIBET TODAY

A **RECORD-BREAKING TWENTY MILLION TOURISTS VISITED TIBET** in 2015, producing some $4.26 billion in tourism revenue. Even though the Chinese government regularly closes Tibet to overseas travelers for five weeks each spring, spanning the anniversary of the 2008 riots in the Tibetan capital Lhasa, and occasionally at other times of periodic unrest, tourism is booming.

Why are millions of people flocking to Tibet? What are they hoping to find there?

For one thing, there is the spectacular scenery. This is the land of the world's highest mountains. Most people find the vistas to be absolutely breathtaking, but in more ways than one. The Tibetan Plateau is the highest region on earth, with an average altitude of 14,760 feet (4,500 meters). Even the capital city, Lhasa, which sits at nearly 12,000 feet (3,650 m), is plenty high enough to cause altitude sickness in visitors who haven't taken the time to acclimate—and even in some who have. The air at such heights is thinner, meaning it has less oxygen, and the body tries to compensate by working harder to get oxygen—the heart pumps faster and breathing is rapid and shallow. Tourists are advised to spend at least three to five days at an altitude between 8,000 to 9,000 feet (2,400 to 2,700 m) before

People walk on Barkhor Street in the old section of Lhasa, Tibet.

heading higher, so their bodies have time to adjust, but not all tourists want to take the time. Altitude sickness, also called acute mountain sickness, can be extremely unpleasant, typically causing a throbbing headache, nausea, exhaustion, and dizziness. Who wants to spend their vacation feeling like that?

Evidently, millions of people are willing to risk altitude sickness, or are willing to add extra time to their travels in order to avoid it. Either way, the region's geography makes visiting more difficult, and snow-capped mountains can be seen at safer altitudes elsewhere. Therefore, something else must draw people to this high, forbidding land.

Tibet has long been regarded as an almost magical place, where people seem to exist on a higher plain, spiritually as well as geographically. Because of its long history of isolation, it's seen as a mysterious, exotic world unlike anywhere else. Buddhism infuses the local culture with a deep sense of serenity and peace that attracts seekers hoping to find an authentic experience.

How, then, to square that image with the reality of monks burning themselves to death in public places to protest Tibet's oppressive rulers?

Something must be profoundly wrong in this magical land. Since 2009, more than 140 Tibetans have self-immolated in protest against Chinese authority. The gruesome protests are intended to call international attention to Tibet's political status as an occupied country whose language and culture are being systematically destroyed.

But is Tibet a country? China insists it is not—Tibet is an administrative region of the People's Republic of China (PRC). The United States and most other countries officially agree. Since 1950, Tibet, or the Tibet Autonomous Region (TAR), has been a part of China—not a country unto itself.

Yet there is another Tibet. Spanning the vast Tibetan Plateau in Central Asia and East Asia, it is the traditional homeland of the Tibetan people. Geographically, this Tibet includes the official Chinese TAR, but is roughly twice as large. This homeland is claimed by the Tibetan "government-in-exile" as the country of Tibet. Its population includes more than one million Tibetans living in exile outside its borders—mostly in India and Nepal.

China has little patience with this group of exiles and their claims. The exile community looks to Tenzin Gyatso, the fourteenth Dalai Lama, who is

A Tibetan woman living in exile shouts anti-China slogans at a 2011 rally in New Delhi, India, following the self-immolation of two monks inside Tibet a few days earlier.

The Dalai Lama speaks to his supporters during a visit to Germany.

an international personality and a symbol for peace. (In 2013, a survey of people in the United States and the five largest European nations found the Dalai Lama to be one of the three most popular leaders in the world, on par with Pope Francis and US president Barack Obama.) In 1959, the Dalai Lama led some one hundred thousand Tibetans out of their homeland to Dharamsala, India, to escape the Chinese, and he has never been allowed back home since. He continues to call for self-rule in his old country. The Chinese are not fans of the Dalai Lama, to put it mildly. Officials and media constantly refer to him as a "splittist" who is trying to incite revolution and violence.

The US State Department has urged China to allow Tibetans to "express grievances freely," while calling on Tibetans to "end self-immolations." Even the Dalai Lama has questioned the effectiveness of the protests, though he points out that dissenting Tibetans could have "easily hurt other people," but instead were choosing "to sacrifice their own lives, not hurting others" in protest.

The Chinese, however, will have none of it. Chinese intentions in Tibet—from their point of view—are for the best. Trying to win American sympathy, Chinese officials have compared themselves to US President Abraham Lincoln. China freed the slaves, they say, referring to the harsh feudal system that existed in Tibet when China took over the country in 1950. Since then, China has been working hard to modernize the once isolated, technologically backward country. Bringing Chinese culture to "backward" Tibet is a gift, from the Chinese point of view. They have merely brought Tibet back into the loving embrace of motherland China, where it rightfully belongs.

However, some Western historians suggest a very different analogy to America's past. The experience of the Tibetans at the hands of the Chinese, they say, is like that of the Native Americans in the face of European settlers centuries ago. After all, the Europeans who first came to the Americas believed they were bringing a superior culture to a backward people, and if the gift needed to be bestowed with an iron hand, then so be it. The Natives would find themselves better off for it, they reasoned.

Carpenters work to restore the four-hundred-year-old Beri Gompa, a seventeenth-century Buddhist monastery in the former Tibetan kingdom of Kham, now in western Sichuan Province, China.

In the American history analogy, the Europeans believed they were saving the souls of the Natives by forcing them to accept Christianity. The Communist Chinese model in Tibet was quite the opposite at first, with the government seeking to eliminate all religion. In the 1960s, Buddhist monasteries and temples were quite literally destroyed, and with it, the Chinese hoped, the Tibetans' Buddhism-based culture. But the Chinese underestimated the depth of the Tibetans' attachment to Buddhism.

Today, the Chinese authorities are more accepting of Buddhism in Tibet, as well as in the rest of China. Certainly the Chinese government recognizes the value of Tibet as a tourist attraction, and to that end has been rebuilding monasteries and encouraging elements of Tibetan culture. However, Tibetan exiles, and those sympathetic to them, charge that China is creating a sort of Disney World version of Tibet, a sort of inauthentic Shangri-La to suit the fantasies of tourists. As long as the pretense of paradise prevails, those observers say, the world will be willing to look the other way at China's human rights abuses and its obliteration of a country, a culture, and a people.

GEOGRAPHY

Snowy mountain peaks tower over the Tibetan landscape.

OFTEN CALLED "THE ROOF OF the world," the land of Tibet is seemingly as much a part of the sky as it is of earth. In keeping with its lofty altitude, perhaps, it has also long been regarded as a mysterious land of the spirit. Tibet is the highest region in the world, with an average altitude of 14,000 feet (4,267 m) above sea level.

Isolated by vast mountain ranges that form its western, northern, and southern borders, it is one of the world's least populated areas. A large portion of the total land area of 474,008 square miles (1,228,000 square kilometers) is uninhabited, barren desert. Tibet is a landlocked region, bounded on the west by India and on the south by Myanmar, India, Bhutan, and Nepal. To the east, it borders the Chinese provinces of Sichuan and Yunnan, and in the north, its neighbors are the Xinjiang Uyghur Autonomous Region of China and the provinces of Qinghai and Gansu.

1

The Northern Plateau has an average elevation of 15,000 feet (4,570 m). Most people who travel to the area experience altitude sickness for the first few days of their visit.

GEOGRAPHIC REGIONS

The Tibetan Plateau encompasses many of the world's highest mountains, including Mount Everest on Tibet's border with Nepal. The Tibetan Plateau is often called earth's "Third Pole," after the North and South Poles. This is because its glaciers and snow-covered mountains hold the world's third-largest store of freshwater ice and permafrost, after the polar regions themselves.

The Tibetan Plateau is often delineated into the lake region in the north and the river region in the east and south.

THE NORTHERN PLATEAU   The Northern Plateau, locally called the Chang Tang, is one of the most inhospitable places on the planet, with low temperatures, high winds, lack of rainfall, and sparse vegetation. It is the largest region of Tibet, covering about half of the Tibet's surface area. The western border is created by the Karakoram Range, which includes K2, the

second-highest peak in the world. To the north lie the Kunlun Mountains. The plateau contains no major rivers and rainfall is sparse, but the lack of drainage on the mountainous plateau has caused salt lakes to develop. This lake region includes Namtso, or Lake Nam, the highest saltwater lake in the world. It is one of three very holy lakes in Tibet—the others being Yamdroktso and Lake Manasarovar. There are some 1,500 lakes in Tibet, both saltwater and fresh.

The Northern Plateau remains largely unexplored. Some of the nomadic people of Tibet make use of the vast plains of the plateau for grazing livestock, but they generally keep to the southern parts of the region where the land is more hospitable.

THE OUTER PLATEAU This great arc of land extends 2,200 miles (3,500 kilometers) west to east in a relatively thin band south of the Northern Plateau. It is bordered to the west by the Karakoram Mountains and to the south by the Himalayas. Through the center runs the great Yarlung Tsangpo River. In the west, the soil is poor and rainfall is low, making agriculture very

Mountains form a backdrop for Lake Namtso, or "Heavenly Lake."

difficult; but farther east in the arc, many of the valleys support a flourishing agriculture. This is because of warmer temperatures, adequate rainfall, and a large supply of river water to irrigate the crops.

The majority of Tibet's small population lives in the Outer Plateau, where most of its cities and towns are located, including Lhasa, the capital and cultural center.

THE SOUTHEASTERN PLATEAU The arc of the Outer Plateau gradually falls in altitude until it reaches the Southeastern Plateau. Here the vegetation is very different and includes dense forests and subtropical plants. The soft sedimentary rocks that characterize this region are deposited in vast ravines and gorges by the large, powerful rivers that originate in Tibet and course southward, nourishing the countries there. The southeastern region is enclosed by the north-south mountain ranges of this area. Between them flow the Yangtze, Mekong, and Salween Rivers. These great rivers flow north to south, almost parallel to one another, with only the mountain ranges separating them. Eventually they emerge in the Chinese provinces of Sichuan and Yunnan.

MOUNTAINS

Himalaya is Sanskrit for "abode of snow." The Himalayas are an enormous chain of mountains that extends from Pakistan eastward across Kashmir, northern India, the southern borders of Tibet, and finally into Nepal, Sikkim, and Bhutan. The Tethys and the Great Himalayas, which form Tibet's southern border, are the two sections of this range in Tibet.

Mount Everest, which rises on the border between Tibet and Nepal, is just one of the vast mountains that form the Great Himalayas. Other well-known Himalayan peaks are Namcha Barwa at 25,445 feet (7,756 m) and Gurla Mandhata at 25,355 feet (7,728 m).

In the west of Tibet lies the Karakoram Range, which stretches all the way into Pakistan. The Nan Shan Range rises to a height of 25,340 feet (7,724 m), dominating the northeastern horizon. Extending 1,500 miles (2,414 km), it forms a natural border between the Northern Plateau and Xinjiang.

MOUNT EVEREST

Chomolungma *or "goddess mother of the world," as the Tibetans call Mount Everest, is the highest point on earth at 29,029 feet (8,848 m) above sea level. Named after Sir George Everest, a surveyor general of India who first recorded the location and height of the mountain, it lies on the border between Tibet and Nepal.*

Attempts to climb the mountain began in 1920 with the opening of the Tibetan access route. However, high altitudes, wind, and cold air resulted not only in failed expeditions, but deaths as well. Tibetan monks were initially reluctant to allow climbers to use the Tibetan route, fearful that the gods of the mountain would kill them. Today, paintings still remain in the now deserted monasteries that depict the fate the monks believed would befall anyone who set foot on the mountain.

When China closed its doors to the outside world in 1951, routes through Nepal were sought. In 1953, Edmund Hillary of New Zealand and Tenzing Norgay of Nepal reached the summit from the southeast ridge. After their success, many more adventurers followed in their footsteps. Today there is a long waiting list of groups wishing to attempt to reach the top. But only a limited number of teams can make the ascent each year because the climbing season is so short and there are very few safe locations for base camps.

By 2012, more than 500 people had reached the summit of Mount Everest, but as of 2016, nearly 280 people have perished on the trek. Climbers die mostly due to avalanches, falls, exposure, or other health problems brought on by extreme conditions on the mountain, including heart attack and high-altitude cerebral edema. Because of the danger and difficulty of retrieving bodies on Everest, people who die on the mountain usually remain there.

WATERWAYS

Many of Asia's most important rivers have their sources in the Tibetan highlands and the neighboring Chinese province of Qinghai. The Indus, which flows northwest across Tibet and into India, forms in western Tibet from the glacial streams of the Himalayas. The Salween forms the border between Myanmar and Thailand before reaching the sea 1,750 miles (2,815 km) from its source in central Tibet.

The Mekong River travels southeast for 2,600 miles (4,185 km) from its source north of Tibet and eventually drains into the South China Sea. The Yangtze flows through huge gorges in southeastern Tibet before traveling south into Yunnan Province. The Huang He, or Yellow River, rises in the Southeastern Plateau and flows east through China where, 2,900 miles (4,667 km) from its source, it empties into the Bohai Sea. Most of Tibet's rivers originate in lakes formed by glacial meltwaters. But on the Northern Plateau, where rainfall is sparse, lake water evaporates very quickly, leaving behind valuable salt deposits.

GLACIERS

The Tibetan Plateau supports some forty-six thousand glaciers, with thirty-seven thousand of those glaciers facing China. In turn, meltwater from these masses of ice feed Asia's mightiest rivers. Some two billion people depend on the waters that originate in these glaciers.

A glacier is produced when snow accumulates and is compressed into ice by the weight of subsequent layers of snowfall. The fluffy snow that falls in the Tibetan mountains is transformed by repeated compression into hard granules, which are covered each year by new fallen snow, burying them deeper and deeper. The weight of the overlying snow then causes the granules to solidify, until there are no air pockets left, eventually creating a solid and compact mass of ice, or a glacier. Once the glacier reaches a depth of about 200 feet (61 m) the lower layers of packed ice become liquid and begin to flow, allowing the glacier to move. This movement erodes mountains, forming sharp, jagged edges and peaks.

Tibet's major waterway, the Yarlung Tsangpo River, is the highest major river in the world. It originates in western Tibet and travels eastward through the South Tibet Valley. It winds through sandbanks, splitting and reforming again, until it reaches Namcha Barwa, a mountain in the east of Tibet. There, it makes a sharp horseshoe turn and runs south into Bangladesh as the Brahmaputra River.

This horseshoe bend in the river forms the Yarlung Tsango Grand Canyon, the deepest and possibly the longest canyon in the world. The canyon plunges 19,714 feet (6,009 m) at its lowest point, and at 314 miles (504.6 km) long, it is longer than the Grand Canyon in the United States. As the river flows through the gorge, it is sometimes called "the Everest of rivers" because of its extreme conditions as it drops some 11,000 feet (3,350 m). Explorers once thought that the sharp drop in altitude was the result of an enormous waterfall, but in 1924 the river was completely mapped and no falls over 30 feet (9 m) were recorded. Instead, the river descends through a series of rapids where the water travels at about 33 feet (10 m) per second.

CLIMATE

Tibet's weather patterns are influenced by its position north of the Himalayas. From June to September, the summer rainfall sweeps across the Indian subcontinent. The rains produce lush vegetation on the southern slopes of the Himalayas, but the northern slopes remain bare and rocky because the mountains are so high that most of the rain never reaches the northern side.

Tibet has a temperate climate with spring beginning in March or April. By midsummer the rainy season has begun, but rainfall is intermittent in the south and the east, and rare in the west and the north. The recorded average rainfall in Tibet is only 15 inches (38.1 centimeters) per year—very low for a region that is dependent on agriculture—so the monsoons are welcomed by the farmers. On the Northern Plateau, where temperatures are very low and winds are very strong, the lack of rain frequently causes dust storms.

By September temperatures drop again, signaling the coming of autumn. Dramatic changes in the weather are not uncommon in summer and autumn when the temperature can drop from 100 degrees Fahrenheit (37.8 degrees Celsius) in the day to below freezing at night. In December the weather turns very cold. On the Northern Plateau, temperatures drop as low as -40°F (-40°C). Winters are cold and dry but very sunny.

FLORA AND FAUNA

Severe weather conditions and high altitudes make it very difficult for any but the hardiest of plants and animals to survive. At the very highest points, permanent snow and ice prevent anything from growing. But just below the snowline, alpine flowers, such as gentians and rock jasmine, flourish. Only plants that can retain moisture and protect themselves from the winds generally survive, so lichens, which are low-lying and grow inside moisture-retaining cushions, form the basic pioneer plants in these regions. The snow leopard and brown bear are typical of animals that thrive in areas at these heights. Birds such as geese, snow pigeons, snow grouse, and griffon vultures also inhabit these parts.

On the Northern Plateau, where grasses dominate the landscape, a different kind of wildlife exists. Wader birds spend the summer months in the salt marshes of the far north. On the higher slopes, the alpine plants appear. Other animals found in this region are wild yaks, feral sheep and goats, wolves, foxes, and snow leopards. These slopes are also home to the chiru, or Tibetan antelope, characterized by its vertical antlers, which can grow up to 28 inches (70 cm) long.

In the southeastern region of the country several species of trees flourish. At these lower altitudes, Tibetan fir, mountain ash, laurel, bamboo, magnolia, and oak are sheltered from the wind and grow to normal heights, unlike the dwarfed trees of the north. Tigers, musk deer, squirrels, macaques, and black bears inhabit these forests.

CITIES AND TOWNS

The total population of the Tibet Autonomous Region, which occupies an area roughly a quarter of the size of the United States, is only about 3.2 million. The majority of the population inhabits the Outer Plateau, living in the administrative center, Lhasa, or in small towns that dot the area. Lhasa is situated in central southern Tibet on a tributary of the Yarlung Tsangpo River. The city stands about 12,070 feet (3,680 m) above sea level and is surrounded by mountains. It is linked to the adjoining provinces of China by modern highways. There are regular flights from the airport outside the capital to Chengdu, Xining, Beijing, Xi'an, Lanzhou, and Chongqing in China.

With a population of about two hundred thousand and a history that dates back 1,400 years, modern Lhasa has become two cities in one—a modern Chinese-built business area juxtaposed against a traditional city that has survived for centuries. The ancient city revolves around the market where traders from all over Tibet meet to barter their goods. Unpaved roads that bend and twist are lined with whitewashed houses.

Lhasa, the capital of Tibet, lies in a valley in the Himalaya Mountains.

Lhasa is the location of three UNESCO World Heritage Sites, which are recognized as one grouping called the Historic Ensemble of the Potala Palace. (For purposes of protection and preservation, the United Nations Educational, Scientific and Cultural Organization (UNESCO) identifies places of cultural and natural heritage around the world that it determines to be of outstanding value to humanity.)

Potala Palace

Norbulingka

Jokhang Temple

The Potala Palace itself is a complex atop Red Mountain which dates to 1645. It was built on the site of an earlier palace constructed in the seventh century, which was the winter residence of the Dalai Lamas until the fourteenth Dalai Lama fled the country in 1959.

About a mile away, the palace of Norbulingka sits on the banks of the Lhasa River in a lush garden environment. It was built in 1755 by the seventh Dalai Lama and served as the traditional summer residence of the Dalai Lamas. In Tibetan, the name Norbulingka *means "Treasure Garden" or "Treasure Park."*

In the old town section of Lhasa, the Jokhang Temple Monastery is the third site within the World Heritage Historic Ensemble. Many Tibetans consider this building, which dates to 652, to be the most sacred temple in Tibet.

According to UNESCO, the three sites together, with their "rich ornamentation and harmonious integration in a striking landscape," exhibit the distinctive characteristics of traditional Tibetan architecture and have "Outstanding Universal Value."

In sharp contrast, the newer part of the city has wide, straight, paved streets lined with planted trees. The modern buildings house government departments, hotels, offices, and apartments. The majority of the ethnic Chinese who live in Tibet make Lhasa their home.

The second-largest city, with a population of about sixty-four thousand, is Shigatse, at an altitude of 12,800 feet (3,900 m). It is situated at the confluence of the Yarlung Tsangpo and Nyang Rivers in the midst of a rich farming area. The town was once dominated by a monastery, but now a modern Chinese-constructed section stands at the center of the town.

Zhanang is southeast of Lhasa and, like other Tibetan towns, has a new Chinese-built section surrounding the older heart of the city. The population here is fast growing due to the expansion of commerce. Zhanang is famous for its pears and apples, which come from nearby orchards.

INTERNET LINKS

www.lonelyplanet.com/china/tibet
This travel site offers photos and information about Tibet's top destinations.

www.tibettravel.com/en/Attractions/Yarlung-Zangbo-Grand-Canyon-4.html
This page features a slideshow and information about the Yarlung Tsangpo Grand Canyon.

whc.unesco.org/en/list/707
This is the UNESCO World Heritage List entry for the Historic Ensemble of the Potala Palace in Lhasa.

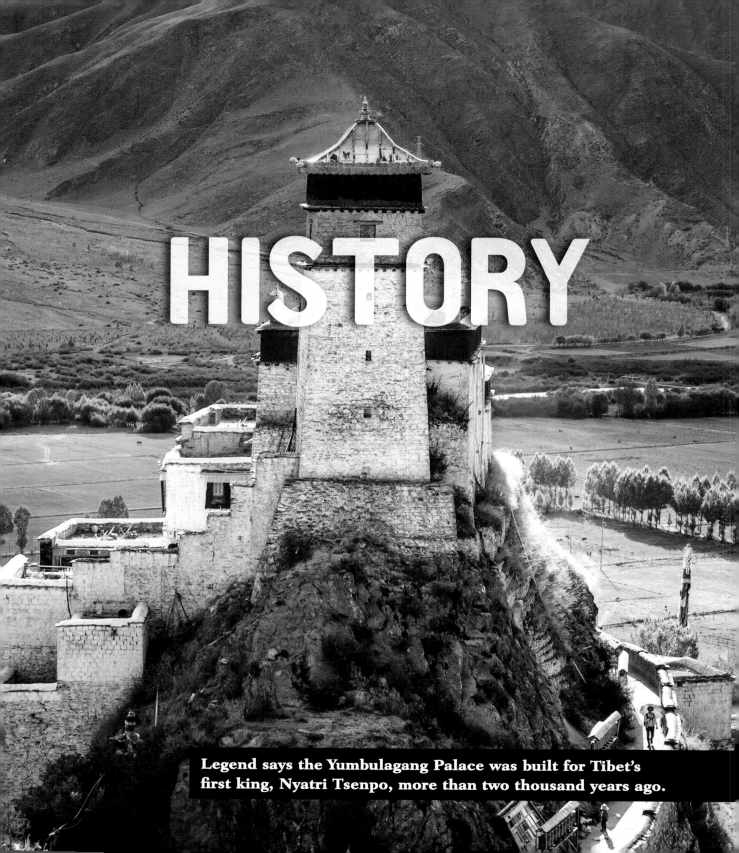

HISTORY

Legend says the Yumbulagang Palace was built for Tibet's first king, Nyatri Tsenpo, more than two thousand years ago.

2

ACCORDING TO FOLKLORE, THE Tibetan people are the descendants of a monkey and a mountain ogress, which is defined in Asian cultures as a demon or a playful sprite. According to the story, the monkey Pha Trelgen Changchup Sempa was an incarnation of the compassionate deity Avalokitesvara (or, in some versions, he was sent by Avalokitesvara). The monkey met the ogress on a mountain in Tibet, and she demanded that he marry her. If he refused, she threatened to marry a devil and spawn countless generations of devils. So the good monkey married the ogress and the couple had six children, who are the ancestors of the Tibetan people.

The first Tibetan king, Nyatri Tsenpo, established the Yarlung dynasty in 127 BCE. (The year of his enthronement marks the first year of the Tibetan calendar.) According to myth, he descended from heaven to become the first ruler of the kingdom, and was therefore hailed as a god. The twenty-six kings who came after him practiced an animistic religion called Bön. In the fourth century CE, during the reign of the twenty-eighth king, legend says that Buddhist scriptures fell from the sky into the king's palace. After Buddhism was introduced to Tibet, the following century was dominated by a conflict between the followers of the two religions.

THE THREE DHARMA KINGS

Three Tibetan kings are particularly credited with establishing Buddhism in Tibet. They ruled during the time of the Tibetan Empire, from the seventh to ninth centuries. In Buddhism, a dharma king is, essentially, king of the dharma. There is no word in English that can be translated as dharma, a Buddhist concept of cosmic law and order. The word also refers to the teachings of Buddha. The dharma kings, therefore, are the important kings who brought Buddhism to Tibet.

SONGTSEN GAMPO Tibet's first great historical leader, Songtsen Gampo (557—649 CE), is the first king whose reign historians can date. He became

Statues of the Tibetan king Songtsen Gampo and his wives adorn the sacred Jokhang Temple, which dates to 652 CE.

the thirty-third king of the Yarlung dynasty at the age of thirteen. He is credited with founding the Tibetan Empire. Prior to his rule, Tibet was divided by warring tribes, and had been virtually ignored by its powerful neighbors: India, Nepal, and China. Under Songtsen Gampo, Tibet became a powerful military and cultural force. In a series of military campaigns and treaties with local chieftains, he took control of a vast region that was bounded by China in the east, the Arab caliphate in the west, and India in the south.

By 648, Songtsen Gampo had invaded northern India and was continuing to expand his empire, threatening China's western border. Rather than oppose him, his neighbors chose to form alliances through marriage, and so the Tibetan king was wed to a Nepalese princess, Tritsun, and a Chinese princess, Wencheng. The dowries of both princesses included lavish statues of the Buddha. Songtsen Gampo is credited with building the Jokhang and Ramoche Temples (which still stand in Lhasa) to house the statues and with giving his official support to the growing religion despite opposition from the followers of Bön.

Songtsen Gampo is revered by Tibetans as a devout Buddhist who built temples and brought the Buddhist scriptures to the Tibetan people. He was also a wise ruler who knew that it was in the country's best interests to learn from its powerful neighbors. Songtsen Gampo is said to have borrowed techniques from each one of them. From the Hor and Yugur peoples of the north, he copied books of law; from China he took books of technology and divinatory calculation; in India he found the means to translate the Buddhist canon into Tibetan, and in the ancient lands of Sok and Nepal, he gained access to foodstuffs, goods, and commercial wealth for his people.

TRISONG DETSEN In the one hundred years following the death of Songtsen Gampo, the Buddhist temples fell into disrepair. The animistic religion practiced by the earlier kings was still a strong force in Tibet, and its priests were jealous of any support the king might give to Buddhism.

Expansion of the empire resumed under the rule of Trisong Detsen (755—797). In 763, Tibetan armies even captured the capital of China, which was then at Chang'an (modern Xi'an), and installed their own emperor. But

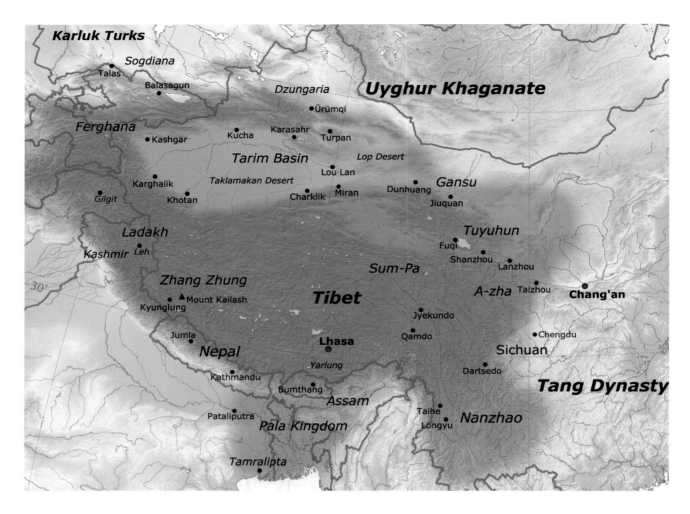

The Tibetan Empire at its greatest extent in the 780s to 790s CE.

Trisong Detsen is remembered in Tibetan history more for his contributions to Buddhism than for his military exploits. Trisong Detsen, a Buddhist himself, restored Songtsen Gampo's temples, invited Buddhist masters into Tibet, and had new translations of the scriptures made. One of the famous monks he brought to Tibet was a man called Shantarakshita, who is revered by modern Tibetans as the Great Abbot Bodhisattva. A bodhisattva is someone who has achieved a state of enlightenment but chooses to return to an earthly life to help other people attain the same state. With

Shantarakshita's help, Trisong Detsen gathered enough support to declare Buddhism the state religion. During his reign, the first Buddhist monastic order was established in Tibet, and the monastery of Samye was built. This angered Bön supporters, who plotted, unsuccessfully, to oust the king from the throne.

RALPACAN In 815, Tritsuk Detsen, or Ralpacan, came to power. He was the forty-first and last of the great Buddhist kings of the Yarlung dynasty of Nyatri Tsenpo. The Tibetan Empire reached its greatest extent under his rule. After years of fighting with neighboring powers, Palpacan signed a peace treaty in 821 with China. A bilingual account of the treaty is inscribed on a pillar outside the Jokhang Temple in Lhasa.

Prior to this, Buddhist scriptures were written in a variety of languages, the most important of which was Sanskrit. Under Ralpacan's rule, regulations were established on how these Buddhist texts should be translated into Tibetan. He also introduced standard weights and measures based on the Chinese system.

Ralpacan was a devoted Buddhist who gave generously to the Buddhist clergy. He himself became a monk. However, the progress of Buddhism did not eliminate earlier beliefs, and in 836 Ralpacan was assassinated by men acting on the orders of his elder brother, Langdarma. Destruction of Buddhist temples and the persecution of Buddhists began immediately after his death. Buddhist scriptures were burned, and monks were forced to leave their order or flee the country. Buddhism was wiped out almost completely during Langdarma's rule.

After six years of persecution, a Buddhist monk in hiding traveled to Lhasa in disguise and shot Langdarma in the heart with an arrow. The monk escaped, but his action brought about the eventual collapse of the Tibetan Empire. Fighting among the potential heirs to the throne split the kingdom into small warring kingdoms. One branch settled in western Tibet and ruled the state of Guge where Buddhism flourished; in the rest of Tibet, Buddhism declined.

THE REVIVAL OF BUDDHISM

The rise and fall of small kingdoms and border disputes with the Chinese continued for four hundred years. In the eleventh century, a group of fugitive monks who had settled in eastern Tibet began secretly restoring the temples and monasteries. Politically, Tibet consisted of a series of small feudal kingdoms, and religion and learning flourished. Daily life among the various peoples of Tibet became closely involved with their religious observances. Leading priests, called lamas, ruled equally with the princes and kings. This period of Tibet's history ended in the thirteenth century with the arrival of Genghis Khan.

THE MONGOLS

In the thirteenth century, the Mongol kingdom dominated China and central Asia. Tibet avoided being attacked early in the century by submitting to the Mongol envoys sent to Tibet. Unconditional surrender meant sending an annual tribute to the Mongol emperor, but in 1240, no tribute was sent.

Under Godan Khan, Genghis's nephew, raiding armies were sent into central Tibet. These attacks halted when the head of the Sakya sect, a Buddhist monastic order established during the revival, was invited to the court of Godan Khan. Legend has it that Sakya Pandita cured the Khan's illness (a skin disease), initiated him into Tibetan Buddhism, and helped create a Mongolian alphabet. In return, Godan Khan granted the Sakya movement the regency of Tibet.

This pact with the Mongols gave the Sakya sect power over the other Buddhist orders. The agreement lasted through the reign of Kublai Khan and continued over the next one hundred years until the decline of the Mongol Empire.

In 1354 the Sakya movement was displaced by Jangchub Gyeltsen, a secular leader aligned with the Kagyu order. In the absence of any real threat from the Mongol Empire, this pattern of secular alignment with the Kagyu order continued for the next three hundred years, until the Yellow Hats, a new order of Buddhist monks who were backed by the Mongols, took control.

While all the political wrangling was going on between the various Buddhist sects during the fourteenth and fifteenth centuries, a new Buddhist religious order was emerging. This was the Gelugpa, or Gelug school, meaning "the virtuous tradition," which is sometimes called the "Yellow Hats." The leader of this sect, Gendun Drupa (1391–1474), testified that when he died, his soul would rise in reincarnation to lead the Yellow Hats.

In 1578, the third incarnation, Sonam Gyatso, was invited to visit the Mongol ruler who gave him the title Dalai Lama, or "ocean of wisdom." The Mongol Empire had declined to some extent, but Mongolia still existed as a potential threat to rival groups in Tibet. With the backing of neighboring Mongolia, the Yellow Hats entered the political arena, and in 1642 the fifth Dalai Lama, Lobsang Gyatso (1617–1682), became the political and spiritual leader of Tibet. This order of Buddhists would control Tibet until the invasion of China in 1950.

THE REIGN OF THE DALAI LAMAS

In the mid-1600s, with the support of the Mongol Empire, Lobsang Gyatso, the fifth Dalai Lama, became the first political and spiritual leader of Tibet. He traveled widely, reforming local governments and encouraging the development of monasteries. Long-term peace and stability led to the emergence of a sense of national identity, while culture and the economy flourished.

Political wrangling began again on the death of the sixth Dalai Lama. In 1717 a group of Mongols attacked Tibet and war broke out. Tibet was looted until the Manchu emperor Kangxi intervened and reinstalled the seventh Dalai Lama, making Tibet a protectorate of China.

For the next two hundred years, Tibet was ruled by a series of regents and councils under the direction of Chinese governors; the Dalai Lamas took little part in politics. The ninth to the twelfth Dalai Lamas all died before reaching eighteen, possibly the result of assassinations. As Tibet entered the nineteenth century it became wary of foreigners and closed its borders to the outside world.

CHINESE "LIBERATION"

Tibet spent most of the nineteenth century closed to outsiders. This isolation was interrupted by a short-lived British invasion in 1904. In 1910, the Manchus invaded to reassert Chinese dominance in Tibet. Under the thirteenth Dalai Lama (1876—1933), Tibet drove the Chinese out of the country in 1911, and Tibet declared its independence.

In China, the Manchu dynasty had collapsed, and the Nationalist and Communist parties were vying for power in a struggle that eventually led to civil war. The Nationalist government fell in 1949, withdrawing to Taiwan, while the Communists took power on the mainland, forming the People's Government Council, headed by Mao Zedong.

One of Communist China's first foreign policy objectives was to "peacefully liberate Tibet." The Chinese People's Liberation Army entered eastern Tibet in 1950, taking control of two provinces. Tibetan appeals to the United Nations were ignored. Left with no other alternative, the Tibetan government negotiated an agreement with the Chinese under which Tibet was to become a part of China while retaining autonomy. The Tibetan people were also free to practice their religion under the leadership of the Dalai Lama.

Not long after the agreement was signed, the Chinese government declared that religion was hampering Tibet's progress. Monasteries were closed and monks were executed or sent out to work in the fields. The centuries-old Tibetan agricultural system was scrapped in favor of a series of collective farms. Chinese citizens were relocated to Tibet in an effort to further the Communist government's policies. A sudden surge in population combined with the inefficient collective farm system led to famine, while the economy collapsed under the burden of an unrealistic reorganization and the demands of the occupying forces.

Small uprisings soon erupted into rebellion when the Communists tried to disarm the Khampas, a nomadic warrior tribe. Fearing arrest by the Chinese government, the Dalai Lama fled to India in 1959. The people of Tibet rose up in protest and thousands were killed.

THE CULTURAL REVOLUTION, 1966—1976

In the 1950s a division began to develop between China's Communist leader Mao Zedong and the country's intellectuals. Under Mao's dictatorship, the Cultural Revolution was inaugurated as a means to root out intellectuals who disagreed with the government and its policies. Under the direction of Mao's government, groups of Chinese youth, known as Red Guards, roamed all over China and its satellite states attacking artists, teachers, doctors, and other professionals and destroying all signs of culture that were deemed to be incompatible with Communist ideals.

Chinese and Tibetan cultural relics were destroyed and hundreds of thousands of people were killed. Most of Tibet's monasteries were destroyed. The Cultural Revolution did not come to an end until the death of Mao Zedong in 1976. Since 1980, the Chinese have restored many of the old monasteries and trained Tibetan artists to create new religious images. The Chinese government opened Tibet for international tourism in the 1980s, but occasionally closes it for "political reasons." China says it has also given Tibetans a greater say in managing their own lives.

After having staged an armed insurrection, Tibetan Buddhist monks surrender to Chinese troops of the People's Liberation Army in April 1959.

TIBET TODAY

China's goal in Tibet continues to be the modernization of the once-isolated, feudal society. To that end, China believes it liberated Tibet from a backward

Internationally, many people consider Tibet an occupied country, and there are numerous organizations dedicated to the need to "Free Tibet." A nonprofit organization called Free Tibet, started in 1987 in London, is one such group; others include the International Campaign for Tibet, established in 1988, and Students for a Free Tibet, founded in 1994 in New York City. These groups and others like them work to raise awareness in the West of China's alleged human rights abuses in Tibet. They pressure China for the release of Tibetan political prisoners. They also encourage cultural resistance among the Tibetan people, cooperate with the exiled Dalai Lama, and work to report unfiltered news from inside Tibet.

A man holds a scarf bearing the slogan "Free Tibet" as supporters of Amnesty International protest against claims of a deterioration in human rights and censorship of the internet and media during a state visit by Chinese President Xi Jinping on October 20, 2015, in London, England.

and oppressive past, and that Chinese culture is a vast improvement. A new railway line linking Lhasa with the western Chinese province of Qinghai has enabled thousands of Han Chinese people to move into Tibet. These people, in turn, have been very influential in turning Tibetan culture and society into an acceptable Chinese version of the same.

However, protests continue against Chinese rule, particularly among Tibetans who remain loyal to the exiled Dalai Lama.

INTERNET LINKS

asianhistory.about.com/od/china/a/TibetandChina.htm
This site offers a history of Tibet, with links to many related articles and photo galleries.

www.bbc.com/news/world-asia-pacific-14533879
"Q&A: China and the Tibetans" offers a clear explanation to common questions about the current situation in Tibet.

www.freetibet.org
www.savetibet.org
www.studentsforafreetibet.org
These are links for organizations working to free Tibet from Chinese governance.

www.pbs.org/wgbh/pages/frontline/shows/tibet/etc/cron.html
Frontline includes a timeline of Tibetan history through the end of the twentieth century.

www.tibetanwarrior.com/index.php/home.html
The English-language website for the Swiss documentary film *Tibetan Warrior* (2015) includes historical information as well as coverage of the protest self-immolations from 2009 to 2014.

GOVERNMENT

Balloons rise over the Potala Palace at a 2015 celebration of fifty years of Chinese rule in Tibet.

3

THE GOVERNMENT OF TIBET IS THE government of China. Although China calls Tibet an "autonomous region," that autonomy is mostly in name only. There is another government of Tibet, which of course China does not recognize, and that government exists outside Tibet's borders and is largely symbolic. Therefore, in order to understand how Tibet's actual government operates, it helps to see it as part of the larger government of China.

THE PEOPLE'S REPUBLIC OF CHINA

The People's Republic of China has a written constitution that has been altered several times since the Communist Party took power in 1949. Under the most recent constitution of 1982, a president is elected for a five-year term by the National People's Congress, the highest body of state power in the country. Executive power lies with the State Council, while the military—a powerful political force in itself—is governed by the Central Military Commission.

The two most powerful positions within the executive are held by the president and by the general secretary of the Communist Party. Decisions affecting the Tibet autonomous area are made in the State Council, where there is no representation by delegates from Tibet.

The legislature, or law-passing body of the Chinese government, is the National People's Congress (NPC), which can also amend the constitution and appoint members of the State Council. The NPC consists of deputies elected for five-year terms from the provinces, autonomous regions, and municipalities of China. In reality the National People's Congress does little more than ratify the decisions of the State Council. Most of the time, the Congress is not convened and is represented by a standing committee.

Tibetan delegates to the People's National Congress have little or no power to change state policy.

Tibetan delegates attend a government meeting at the Great Hall of the People in Beijing, China.

LOCAL GOVERNMENT

Tibet is administered as an autonomous region divided into seven prefectures, which in turn are organized into sixty-eight counties, and five districts. Local governing bodies are the Tibet Communist Party Committee and the People's Government. The party's secretary is the leader of the Communist Party in Tibet, and the most powerful government official in the region. In 2016, this position was held by Chen Quanguo, an ethnic Chinese. Chen had never lived in Tibet until his assignment there as party chief in 2011. Under him is the chairman of the Tibet Autonomous Region, who is something like a governor. That person is usually an ethnic Tibetan; in 2016, it was Losang Jamcan.

Below this umbrella structure, Tibet is organized into smaller village units where party discussion groups can put forward ideas and suggestions to improve village life. However, critics claim that village units have little or no power, and that Tibet is actually governed by a massive bureaucracy, whose policies are supported by the enormous military presence.

When the Dalai Lama fled Tibet for India in 1959, nearly one hundred thousand Tibetans joined him in the months that followed. The community of refugees was granted political asylum by the Indian government but was refused international aid for fear of escalating the Cold War, already at its height. The Dalai Lama appealed for international aid on several occasions. Eventually the United Nations demanded "respect for human rights of the Tibetan people."

Turning to the Buddhist precepts of patience and endurance, the Dalai Lama established a community of learning in Dharamsala, while waiting for the day when he could return to his people in Tibet. Monasteries and Tibetan Buddhist schools are currently fully active; they also welcome visitors and students from Tibet and other countries.

Lobsang Sangay, leader of the Tibetan government-in-exile, casts his vote in the 2016 election. He was reelected for another five years.

The Dalai Lama resigned his political duties in 2011, but the government-in-exile continues. Today it is called the Central Tibetan Administration (CTA), headed by the kalon tripa (prime minister) Lobsang Sangay, who was elected in 2011. The CTA has a government-like structure, with a cabinet of ministers, a parliament, and democratic elections held every five years. However, it is not recognized as a sovereign government by any country, and the CTA itself claims its mission is not to take power in Tibet. Rather, it will dissolve itself "as soon as freedom is restored in Tibet" and a new government is formed inside the country by Tibetans themselves.

Meanwhile, the CTA oversees the welfare of the Tibetan exile community in India, who number about one hundred thousand. Some one thousand refugees flee to this community each year from China, usually by way of Nepal.

PEOPLE'S JUDICIARY

The highest body in the judicial system is the Supreme People's Court. It is responsible for upholding the constitution and regulations of the State Council. The 1982 constitution of China guarantees the right of legal defense to those brought to the official law courts. However, the way the justice system operates in Tibet is very different from what is commonly practiced in other countries. Most of the cases that elsewhere would be handled in the courts are brought instead to the Communist Party at its local meetings. Issues such as minor theft and divorce are dealt with in this way. Although trials are held, in many cases these are for the purpose of making an example for the public. For many years, those found guilty were summarily dealt with, without the right of appeal.

Today the Chinese authorities have introduced a number of changes to make the judicial process more accessible. For example, court proceedings are now regularly televised, and verdicts are published on the internet. However, some critics argue that political dissidents and religious leaders in the country are still not given fair trials by international standards.

CHINESE VERSUS TIBETAN RULE

For many years Tibet existed as an independent state with its own national language, religion, and culture. But in many ways the country was run as a feudal state with no recognition or representation of the people. There was no constitutional guarantee of human rights, and judiciary sentences were often harsh and arbitrary.

Although it is arguable whether the Chinese administration brought greater freedom to the Tibetans, the Chinese government has built roads and power stations, developed industry, and encouraged tourism in Tibet. Many Tibetans now have a better standard of living than they did under the rule of the Dalai Lamas. They have access to consumer goods, television and radio, and limited religious freedom. Many monasteries, damaged or destroyed during the Cultural Revolution, have been restored and declared national monuments, and modern homes and offices have been built.

But the same administration also encourages hundreds of thousands of Chinese settlers to migrate to the region with offers of guaranteed jobs with higher pay, preferential education for their children, and newly built homes. It also sends thousands of Tibetan children out of the region to schools in Chinese provinces, where they learn to speak Chinese more fluently than Tibetan. This consequent cultural erosion greatly concerns the Tibetan government-in-exile. The Dalai Lama has made overtures to the Chinese administration, hoping for some improvements for his people, but most of these have been rejected. Many international human rights organizations have also repeatedly accused the Chinese government of violating the political rights and civil liberties of the Tibetan people.

INTERNET LINKS

www.constituteproject.org/constitution/China_2004.pdf?lang=en
This is an English-language PDF of the constitution of the People's Republic of China.

eng.tibet.cn/index.shtml
China Tibet Online offers up-to-date China-centric Tibetan information, including governmental positions and perspectives.

www.theatlantic.com/magazine/archive/1999/02/tibet-through-chinese-eyes/306395
This article offers a very insightful look at the Chinese perspective on Tibet.

tibet.net
This is the home site of the Central Tibetan Administration, the government-in-exile, in English.

ECONOMY

A car exits the Galongla Tunnel at the opening of the Metok Highway in 2010.

4

WHEN CHINA INVADED IN 1950, Tibet was an isolated and mostly self-sufficient country with an agricultural economy. The Chinese claim Tibetans lived in abject poverty, many of them essentially slaves trapped in a cruel, feudal serfdom. Much of that may have been true. However, Western academics argue about the accuracy of the Chinese socioeconomic portrayal of early twentieth-century Tibet. Records are few, and a great deal of what is known is based on individual observations and reports. Nevertheless, most historians agree that pre-China Tibet was no Shangri-La, as some Western imaginations would like to believe.

Before China's intervention, Tibet was a premodern agricultural society with minimal economic development. There were no roads, and the only form of transportation was by horse or donkey. Wheeled

In 2010, Tibet's Metok County, with a population of eleven thousand, became the final county in China to become accessible by highway. The 2-mile long (3,310 m) Galongla Tunnel, constructed under extremely difficult conditions at an altitude of 12,303 feet (3,750 m), completed the Metok Highway project. The highway now connects previously isolated Metok, in Nyingchi Prefecture, to Bome County.

vehicles didn't even exist in the country until the twentieth century. When they did arrive, this new form of transportation consisted of only two cars (reserved for the use of the Dalai Lama), both of which had been dismantled and brought into Tibet on horseback through the mountain passes. There was no electricity, no telephone service, no radio, and little contact with the outside world.

Small, mobile family units raised cattle and sheep and grew crops. As the seasons changed, these families moved with their animals to find more suitable grazing land. A delicate balance existed between this vast inhospitable land and the people who made a living from it. In a country where firewood is not plentiful, animal dung was dried and used as fuel, leaving little or none to use for fertilizing crops. Due to the lack of trade, population growth in Tibet was determined by the amount of resources that could be extracted from the land. The importance of religion in Tibet also meant that large numbers of men and women devoted their lives to service in nunneries and monasteries.

Today's Tibet is a very different place.

THE ARRIVAL OF THE CHINESE

When the Chinese arrived, they instituted changes that worked in other parts of China. They banned the barter system, which was the method by which most Tibetans obtained necessities, and replaced it with Chinese currency. Winter wheat was introduced as the major crop in a land whose economy depended on barley, and small farms were transformed into communes. The communes raised large herds of animals, which grazed on a few plots of land.

But Tibet is not like other parts of China. As a result of these changes, the soil quickly became barren, leading to serious crop failures and periods of famine. In 1980, Hu Yaobang, the chairman of the Chinese Communist Party, visited Tibet and was shocked at conditions there. As a result, the communes were disassembled, herds were broken up and redistributed, and the winter wheat policy was abandoned. Trade with Nepal was allowed again, and tourists were granted visas to enter Tibet. Recently, China has been investing heavily in the Tibet Autonomous Region and Western China.

INVESTMENT IN TIBET'S ECONOMY

By 2015, the Chinese government had invested more than 648 billion yuan ($100 billion) in Tibet. In a massive push to update the undeveloped region, the government funded huge power and transportation projects, including the Zangmu hydropower station on the Yarlung Tsangpo River, which became fully operational in October 2015. In 2014, China completed an important 156-mile (251 km) rail link between Tibet's capital, Lhasa, and Shigatse, its second-largest city.

The Zangmu Hydropower Station, Tibet's largest hydropower facility, began generating electricity in 2014.

Heavy Chinese subsidies have pushed the Tibet Autonomous Region's economy into double-digit growth. The numbers are impressive. Its growth has averaged 12.4 percent annually in the twenty-first century, which is higher than China's already impressive national average of 10 percent. But then, as China's poorest region, Tibet has far to go to catch up with the rest of the country.

Critics say China's massive subsidies may be improving the economic scene in the region in general, but they aren't benefiting the Tibetan people as a whole. Rather, the beneficiaries of the improvements are mainly the thousands of Han Chinese who have moved there. These are the people who work in the construction and tourism industries while the majority of Tibetans still make their living as herders and farmers.

AGRICULTURE

Tibet still has a largely agricultural economy. Its principal crops are grown in the fertile southern part of the country and include barley, oats, rapeseed, corn, and buckwheat. Legumes such as broad beans and peas, which are useful in fertilizing the soil, are grown in the south. Mustard and many green vegetables are also cultivated. Small amounts of cotton, soybeans, and hemp are grown commercially.

Vegetables grow in tidy fields in rural Tibet.

The high altitude and intense sunshine allow for two harvests a year, each giving enormously high yields. As much as 5,350 pounds of barley per acre (2,429 kilograms per hectare) can be harvested in Tibet as opposed to an average yield of 1,780 pounds per acre (807 kg/ha) elsewhere.

The introduction of technology has also contributed substantially to the high crop yield. Land once farmed entirely by yak-drawn wooden plows is now tilled by tractors and other modern machines. Irrigation systems and reservoirs have been built to make up for inadequate rainfall.

During Mao's regime farmers were given quotas and the produce was collected by the regional government for redistribution. Now farmers are free to make their own contracts and sell to the highest bidders.

Animal husbandry is also practiced widely in Tibet. In the northern regions of the country herders are largely nomadic, moving with their animals in search of fresh grazing land. The yak is the most common animal in these parts, but goats, sheep, horses, donkeys, and a yak-cow cross called a *dzo* (ZO) are also kept. Wool from sheep is the most important article of trade for these pastoral nomads.

MINERALS

There is always a geological survey or two in progress somewhere in Tibet, seeking to uncover greater mining opportunities. Previous surveys have indicated that there are large deposits of minerals and other natural resources in Tibet; these include iron ore, coal, oil, shale, manganese, lead, zinc, and graphite. Gold, jade, and other precious and semiprecious stones have also been found. China has been steadily developing Tibet's mining industry in order to exploit these resources and channel them for use in its

YAKS

Yaks are native to the Central Asian plateau. The vast majority of yaks are found in the Himalaya region and farther north toward Mongolia and Russia. Wild male yaks are about 6.5 feet (2 m) high at the shoulder and weigh up to about 2,200 pounds (1,000 kg). They are covered with long black or brown hair, and have long horns and a hump on their shoulders. They are well adapted to high altitudes, and have larger lungs and hearts than other kinds of cattle.

Domesticated yaks are smaller, and their coats range from black to red or white. They are enormously useful to the Tibetans. These animals produce rich milk that can be made into cheese and butter; the butter can also be used as fuel. The meat is eaten raw, dried, or roasted. The bones are made into jewelry or utensils and the hide and fur can be fashioned into clothing, rope, boats, or tents. A dzo, a cross between a yak and a cow, is a smaller, more docile animal often used to pull plows.

other developing provinces and cities. Small amounts of salt and borax have been collected for years, but there is a potential to develop these operations into significant industries. The world's largest lithium deposit is in Tibet, and uranium deposits have also been found.

MANUFACTURING

Manufacturing in Tibet is still somewhat in its infancy, even when compared with the less developed parts of China. When early attempts at industrializing Tibet failed, the Chinese realized they had to first build up the region's infrastructure and train the local population in work habits that support such an economy.

Today, mining, construction materials, handicrafts, and Tibetan medicine are growing industries. Carpets and textiles, especially wool, are among the principal items manufactured. Other manufactured goods include processed leather, chemicals, and electrical equipment, mostly for home consumption. Traditional Tibetan handicrafts are popular with tourists and even other Tibetans, and are seen as a positive step toward revitalizing Tibetan culture. Those engaged in handicraft work are entitled to state subsidies. The tourism industry and all the related goods and services that go along with it are booming.

THE MILITARY

The military is probably the largest single employer in Tibet. There are an estimated several hundred thousand well-armed People's Liberation Army troops in Tibet, with numerous military camps surrounding Lhasa alone. Compared with the fourteen military airfields, there is only one civilian airfield. Intercontinental ballistic missiles are kept at bases scattered across the region. Tibet is strategically important for China, as it acts as a forward base for any potential attack on China's neighbors and forms a natural barrier to any invasion or missile attack from that area. Tibet is also used as a nuclear testing site.

FORESTRY

Timber is the largest export from Tibet into China. Although most of Tibet is covered with grasslands, in the valleys of the southeast several species of evergreen and deciduous trees can be found. In the tropical zones camphor and tropical oaks produce valuable hardwoods. The tung tree, which produces resin-like oil, and a lacquer tree that yields varnish are also harvested.

TOURISM

In 1981 Tibet was reopened for tourism. At the same time, the government allowed for the restoration of some monasteries and holy places, an effort generally undertaken by returning monks and their supporters. At first the mostly undeveloped infrastructure could not support the large numbers of tourists necessary to make tourism a viable industry. Only in recent years have luxury hotels, bus services, and restaurants started appearing in Tibetan cities. A small handicraft industry that began by selling cultural and religious items such as prayer wheels and ethnic jewelry to tourists has grown tremendously.

In 2012, more than 10 million domestic and foreign tourists visited the Tibet Autonomous Region, up from 8.69 million in 2011 and 6.85 million in 2010. The government reports that some three hundred thousand people work in the region's tourism sector.

Although tourism will continue to bring in foreign currency, facilitate cultural exchange, and help spur the development of Tibet's infrastructure, some worry there is a danger that it will be at the cost of that which Tibetans have been fighting to protect—their ancient culture and religious beliefs.

INTERNET LINKS

www.eastasiaforum.org/2015/07/09/tibets-economic-growth-an-accounting-illusion
This article asserts that Tibet's economic growth figures are misleading.

www.economist.com/topics/tibet
The Economist lists links to its many articles about Tibet.

english.chinatibetnews.com/xwzx/Economy
This China-centric site reports the economic news from the TAR.

ENVIRONMENT

Snow leopards, such as this young animal, live in the high mountains of Central Asia.

5

THE ENVIRONMENTAL SITUATION in Tibet is often seen as a choice between ecological protection and economic development. Due to its years of isolation, pre-China Tibet had a pristine environment. China's ambition in this region has always been modernization. Rapid development is almost always accompanied by damage to the natural surroundings, and in China, environmental awareness has come late.

After Tibet was annexed, the Chinese government tried to change the Tibetans' traditional way of life by imposing many new social and economic policies. However, it failed to consider how these policies would affect the environment. As a result, the natural landscape and ecology were severely damaged. As part of China's attempt to modernize the Tibetan economy, for instance, it introduced farming practices, such as collective farming, that went against the age-old tried and tested agricultural and pastoral practices of the Tibetans. As a result, the agricultural lands became significantly less productive, livestock numbers decreased, and extreme food shortages occurred.

In addition, severe deforestation and desertification happened in areas where the government approved extensive clearing of forests in order to supply timber to other parts of China. The natural landscape was

The bharal, or Himalayan blue sheep, is one of the endangered animals living in Tibet's mountainous lands.

thus changed quite dramatically, causing alarm both within Tibet as well as among environmentalists all over the world.

In the 1990s the Chinese government began to have a change of heart. After experiencing the negative impact of its policies, government officials began to see the need to protect the fragile ecological balance in Tibet, as well as to prevent further damage to the natural environment. Since then, it has launched numerous environmental projects have been launched. Many of these programs are expected to run until 2050.

Nevertheless, environmental oversight is limited, particularly in economically high-stakes areas such as mining, which can devastate local air, water, and soils. Chinese officials are rarely forthcoming about industrial accidents and pollution statistics.

BIODIVERSITY

Tibet is home to many species of wildlife. According to some scientists, it is even comparable to the Amazon rain forest in terms of its rich biodiversity, with around 210 known species of mammals and hundreds of bird species in the region. Rare birds living in Tibet include the endemic black-necked crane, Tibetan snowcock, tragopan, Tibetan eared pheasant, and Tibetan sand grouse. Some of these animals have become endangered due to the destruction of their habitats by mining or logging activities. Endangered mammals include the snow leopard, white-lipped deer, Himalayan black bear, blue sheep, golden monkey, and Tibetan gazelle.

The land is also home to an array of plant life, some twelve thousand species, ranging from microscopic fungi to huge trees that are hundreds of years old. Nearly two thousand distinct plant species have also been found to

be of medicinal value. Scientists believe that significant advances in medicine could be made if they were properly studied.

In recent years, many larger animals have been threatened by poaching and unlicensed hunting. Despite the country's strict wildlife conservation laws, poachers continue to be active throughout Tibet, targeting mammals such as wild yaks for their hides, antlers, fur, bones, and meat. These animal parts are illegally transported outside Tibet, often to China, to be processed, before being exported around the world. Exotic birds are also hunted, stuffed, and displayed as trophies.

In some places it is common to see groups of tourists heading into the forests for recreational hunting. This is illegal, but due to a lack of manpower, the authorities are sometimes unable to hire enough rangers to stop them. These hunters are generally wealthy tourists from abroad who are looking for exotic trophies to decorate their homes.

A customs official in Lhasa displays confiscated wild animal skins. Poaching for illegal trade is a leading cause of endangered species.

TIBETAN ANTELOPE

The Tibetan antelope, or chiru, lives in the high altitudes of the Tibetan Plateau. Unfortunately for this native Tibetan mammal, it has an extremely soft, wool undercoat called shahtoosh, which can be woven into luxurious textiles. Shawls made from this material are highly prized and can sell internationally for thousands of dollars.

During the last two decades of the twentieth century, the chiru population declined by more than 50 percent and the species is now endangered. Much of this decline is due to poaching for its fur. Although the animal's fur can be obtained without killing it, poachers find it faster and easier simply to kill the creature. It takes about four chiru to make one shawl. Today, the selling of products containing shahtoosh is illegal, but of course, it still occurs.

NATURAL RESOURCES

Since the late 1970s the extraction of many of Tibet's natural resources has been intensified to fuel industrial development throughout China. Besides having among the largest deposits of uranium and borax in the world, as well as significant supplies of other minerals such as lithium, copper, iron, and gold, geological surveys have also detected deposits of corundum, vanadium, titanium, magnesite, sulphur, mica, cesium, rubidium, arsenic, graphite, lepidolite, and potash.

China has invested huge amounts of money in developing the mining infrastructure necessary to gain access to these resources and to channel them to other parts of China. As a result, the natural landscape has changed tremendously, threatening the fragile ecological balance in Tibet.

DEFORESTATION

Tibet's forests are some of the oldest in the whole of central Asia. They are largely clustered in the eastern and southern regions of the country, with spruce, fir, pine, larch, cypress, birch, and oak trees growing up and down the steep slopes of the mountainous terrain. Before Tibet was absorbed by China, its forests occupied an area of 85,637 square miles (221,800 sq km). This area remained untouched because it was largely uninhabited, and very little logging was carried out. Many of the trees had stood for centuries.

Toward the latter half of the twentieth century, Tibet's forestland shrank drastically to only 51,737 square miles (134,000 sq km), due to logging as well as road-building projects. As these projects were seen to be vital to the country's economy, little thought was given to the environmental consequences. In time, desertification and soil erosion made the area prone to landslides and floods, which further transformed the landscape. These environmental changes resulted in the severe flooding of the Yangtze River in 1998, an event that is regarded by China as a national disaster. The number of people who lost their lives due to the floods was reported by some to be as high as ten thousand. In total, over two hundred million people were affected. The following year, four hundred people lost their lives in a similar flood, and sixty-six million people were directly affected.

In response to these disasters the Chinese government began to implement measures to conserve the forests, even to the extent of banning logging in certain parts of Tibet as well as in neighboring provinces.

POLLUTION

Another worrisome result of Tibet's rapid development is the pollution of its rivers. In many parts of the world, rivers sometimes serve as a convenient, if illegal, dumping ground for industrial and chemical waste, and it is no different in Tibet.

Environmentalists are especially concerned about radioactive pollution from the country's uranium mines. Due to inexperience and ignorance, landfill sites meant to contain radioactive waste from the mines are often not properly lined before they are used, and as a result the waste ends up contaminating the whole surrounding area, including the soil and water sources. Some environmentalists have even claimed that Tibetans living near a uranium mine in the neighboring province of Qinghai had died from consuming contaminated water.

ENERGY

Tibet is blessed with many renewable power resources such as solar energy and geothermal energy. However, the Chinese government's exploitation of hydroelectricity in Tibet has come under fire from environmentalists.

Since the 1990s, a number of hydroelectric stations have been built along Tibet's rivers, especially on the Yarlung Tsangpo River. As the output from these power stations far exceeds the needs of Tibetans, the excess electricity is exported to more developed Chinese provinces and cities. The construction of these power stations, however, has resulted in changes to the course of the rivers and, consequently, the vegetation that relies on the rivers for its water supply. These changes have adversely affected the traditional lifestyles of many nomadic communities, and have also destroyed the natural habitats of many animal species.

The Chinese authorities have also looked into harnessing solar and geothermal power in Tibet. An example of their efforts is the Yangbajain Geothermal Power Station near Lhasa, which was one of the largest facilities of its kind when it was launched in 1988. At full capacity it can supply up to 40 percent of Lhasa's electricity needs. Other geothermal power stations scattered around the country have given rural Tibetans access to electricity in their homes.

Solar energy is another practical option for Tibetans living in rural areas. There are approximately one hundred thousand solar furnaces in use in Tibet, and many houses are now being built with solar-powered systems for heating water. Thanks to this relatively accessible and economical source of energy, rural communities have been able to reap the benefits of using electrical appliances in their daily lives.

CONSERVATION

Tibetans traditionally have great regard for the natural environment. This is largely based on Buddhist teachings, which discourage people from destroying the environment as this might harm other living creatures that make their homes in the area. As far back as 1642, the Dalai Lama issued regular reminders for Tibetans to care for their natural surroundings.

In more recent times, the Chinese government has begun to recognize the need to protect the environment, especially after it witnessed first-hand the devastating repercussions of environmental degradation. Since 1996 many environmental projects have been launched by the government, including forest protection schemes, farmland restoration programs, wildlife protection campaigns, and the establishment of nature reserves. It is estimated that these programs will cost the Chinese government as much as 22 billion yuan ($2.7 billion). Despite the cost, these schemes are an important and worthwhile step toward protecting and sustaining the environmental heritage of Tibet.

INTERNET LINKS

meltdownintibet.com/f_solutions.htm
This article details China's recent efforts to build hydroelectric and solar power facilities in Tibet.

www.nature.com/news/double-threat-for-tibet-1.15738
This article assesses the effects of climate change and development on Tibet's environment.

wildtibet.org/tibet-wildlife-directory.htm
This site lists the species that live in Tibet.

wwf.panda.org/what_we_do/endangered_species/tibetan_antelope
This is the World Wildlife Fund page about the Tibetan antelope.

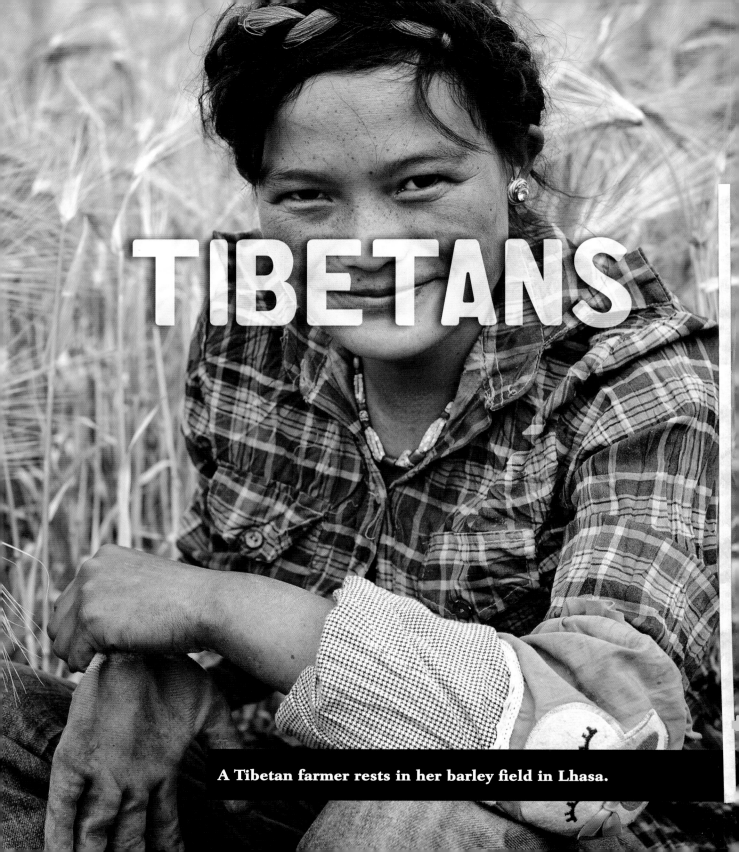

TIBETANS

A Tibetan farmer rests in her barley field in Lhasa.

6

THE CHINESE CONSIDER TIBETANS an ethnic minority in China. The population of China itself, according to the 2010 census, is 91.5 percent Han, the main Chinese ethnicity. The Han people therefore see Tibetan people—which the Chinese refer to as the Zang people— as one of the fifty-five ethnic minority groups that constitute the remaining 8.5 percent of the Chinese population. These ethnic peoples tend to live in the border or frontier regions of China. This includes the Tibet Autonomous Region (TAR). From that perspective, Tibetans account for less than 0.5 percent of China's population. The Chinese government insists that all minorities have "regional ethnic autonomy" and the "right of self-government to administer local affairs and the internal affairs of their own ethnic groups."

In 2014, the Chinese government began promoting intermarriage between Han Chinese and Tibetans, in some cases with cash payments and other favors. The goal of the drive is to "promote ethnic unity," though critics charge that the real purpose is to eliminate Tibetan identity.

A smiling woman and her granddaughter wear traditional clothing on a summer's day in rural Tibet.

The number of Tibetans in Tibet is a difficult number to pin down. For one thing, it depends on one's definition of Tibet. The 2010 Chinese census reports that 90 percent of the 3 million people living in the TAR are ethnic Tibetans. The International Campaign for Tibet puts the number of Tibetans at 6 million, but uses a larger map of Tibet proper. The Unrepresented Nations and Peoples Organization (UNPO), of which the Tibet government-in-exile is a member, says greater Tibet has an estimated population of 6 million Tibetans and 7.5 million Chinese "settlers." Looked at from that perspective, Tibetans are a minority in their own country—or what was their own country. In 2008, the Dalai Lama called the increasing movement of Han Chinese people into Tibet "demographic aggression," and called the population shift a "form of cultural genocide."

It's also very difficult to track the numbers of Tibetans in the region relative to when the Chinese "liberated" or "invaded" the country. This statistic is unknown largely because isolated, pre-Chinese Tibet did not have a census of its population. Any figure claimed for the demographics at that time is purely guesswork.

THE HAN CHINESE

Figures for the total number of ethnic Chinese living in Tibet vary enormously from about seven million according to the Tibetan government-in-exile to about 250,000 according to the Chinese authorities. (Again, the wide gap can perhaps also be attributed to the difference between "Tibet" and the Tibet Autonomous Region.) Whatever the actual figure, it is most likely to be high in comparison with the Tibetan population. In fact, in the cities and larger towns the Chinese population exceeds the Tibetan.

Ethnic or Han Chinese people have many reasons for choosing to live in Tibet. They are guaranteed good jobs with higher pay than they would get elsewhere in China, their children are given priority in education, and they live in modern Chinese-built houses. If they choose to start their own businesses, they receive state subsidies and tax breaks.

NATIVE TIBETANS

The people who have traditionally inhabited Tibet are thought to be the descendants of a non-Chinese race who came to Tibet from the northeast and who had intermarried with the Chinese. In addition, there are smaller groups of varying ethnic origin: the Monba (sometimes spelled Monpa or Menpa), who look different from most Tibetans and who speak in a different tongue; the Bhotia, who generally live outside Tibet around the Tibet-Nepal border; and the Ladakhi, who now largely live in eastern Kashmir but who consider themselves Tibetan.

The people in the various geographical areas of Tibet have different legends surrounding their origins: the people of the central valleys claim that the southeast is the birthplace of the Tibetans, while aristocratic families believe that they originated in the north and northeast of the country, closer to the borders with China. Whatever their origins, Tibetans are generally characterized by their lifestyle—the Bopa, or settled people of the south and east, and the Drokpa, nomadic people of the Northern Plateau.

THE BHOTIA

Bhot is the name by which Tibet is known to the Nepalese and the Indians. The Bhotia are seasonal nomads who speak Tibeto-Burman dialects and who practice Tibetan Buddhism (Lamaism). Physically, they resemble Tibetans, and for the most part they consider themselves to be Tibetan even though a large majority of them actually live in the areas of India and Nepal that border Tibet. During the agricultural season, they live in furnished houses built of stone and timber.

A nomadic Tibetan woman milks a yak.

Like the Tibetans, the Bhotia depend heavily on the yak for food, clothes, fuel, and the tents they use during the grazing season, as well as for implements made from its bones and hooves. In addition to yaks, they also raise sheep and goats. Their characteristic dress is similar to the traditional Tibetan style—long woolen clothes with lots of jewelry. The old Tibetan tradition of polyandry (one woman taking more than one husband, usually brothers) is still common among them, and there is considerable gender equality between Bhotia men and women.

For many years, until the Chinese relaxed restrictions on the practice of religion, the Bhotia were one of the few communities who were able to keep the traditions of Tibetan Buddhism alive.

THE LADAKHI

The Ladakhi are another Tibetan group who live outside the borders of Tibet, in the Jammu and Kashmir state of India on Tibet's western border. Ladakh is sometimes called "Little Tibet," because of the strong influence of Tibetan culture. There are about 270,000 Ladakhi living on the Ladakh Plateau.

Ethnic Ladakhi speak a Tibetan dialect. About half of them practice Tibetan Buddhism, while the other half are Tibetan Muslims. They are the descendants of Tibetans who moved west out of Tibet and mixed with other ethnic groups, such as the Dards and the Mons of ancient Kashmir. In dress, they are similar to the nomads of northern Tibet—they often wear felt boots, leggings, and a woolen or sheepskin greatcoat.

Like the Bhotia, the Ladhaki women often marry all the brothers of one family. Many of the men enter monasteries, joining the Buddhist sect popularly known in Tibet as the Kagyu school of Tibetan Buddhism, the rivals of the followers of the Lamas.

The Ladakhi were greatly affected when the borders of Tibet were closed because they are pastoralists and traders who often crossed the border to trade in Tibet. Today their livelihoods are threatened as the roads are open to modern transportation, which is far more efficient than their yaks. The Ladhaki live very much as the pastoral Tibetans do, farming crops such as cereals that they irrigate by means of terracing and trapping water from mountain streams. The men do most of the plowing, while the women look after the crops once they have been planted. During the summer most of the men travel with the animals to better grazing lands, just as the pastoral Tibetans do.

Ladhaki homes are built into the sides of mountains in split levels. Houses have flat roofs and have very few, if any, windows. Family members sleep together on a raised platform at the back of the house. The *chuba* (CHOO-pa) is the traditional Ladhaki outer garment for all men, while the women also wear a striped skirt and striped apron, woolen leggings, and felt boots. Like Tibetans, Ladhaki women braid their hair to reflect their marital status.

THE LHOBA

Although the Lhoba (or Luopa) live in southeastern Tibet, few of them speak Tibetan, preferring their own ancient language, which has no written form. They rely primarily on agriculture for their livelihood, but they also keep animals, produce textiles, and hunt. Like Tibetans, they adorn themselves with jewelry. The men wear sleeveless jackets made of wool and hats made of bearskin or bamboo. The women wear short blouses with a round neckline and narrow sleeves, and a close-fitting skirt. Unlike most other Tibetan Buddhists, the Lhoba always bury their dead in the ground.

THE MONBA

The Monba represent a population of about twenty-five thousand in the TAR, though statistics vary greatly depending on source. They are concentrated primarily in the forested areas around the Monyul area in southern Tibet. Although they depend on agriculture, they are also engaged in forestry, animal husbandry, and hunting. Their diet consists mainly of the grains they grow: rice, chicken-claw millet, corn, and buckwheat. Monba houses are built of stones or rocks with pointed roofs that look like an inverted "V". These are two to three stories high; living quarters are upstairs, while the animals are kept downstairs. The Monba are easily distinguished by their red pulu robe and black felt hat with a brown top, an orange fringe, and a gap at its peak. The women generally wear white aprons at their waists and carry yak hides on their backs to keep out the cold.

SOCIAL HIERARCHIES

Tibetan social hierarchies are very complicated and made even more so by the overlay of Chinese values that has permeated society since the 1950s. When the Chinese arrived in Tibet they expected to find a feudal society where an aristocratic class ruled over peasants and artisans. This was true only to a certain extent, as the situation was somewhat more complicated.

Aristocratic Tibetan families traced their descent from the early royal Tibetan families who had migrated to central Tibet from the east and northeast. Peasants and nomads lived a hard life working for the nobles or tending to their own small farms. But accompanying this feudal structure was also a powerful religious order that joined the aristocracy at the apex of Tibetan society.

Estimates put the number of monks and nuns before 1950 at 20 percent of the total population. Within the monasteries, monks were divided by rank and function. In each sect, monks took on different roles, many of them being more involved with the everyday running of the monastery than religious devotion. In the past, the country was run jointly by the monks and the nobility.

But unlike other feudal societies where one's rank at birth remained unchanged throughout one's lifetime, the monastic system allowed for a degree of social mobility. Most families dedicated one of their children to the monasteries, where they were fed, clothed, educated, and employed. The priesthood offered the children of the poor the opportunity to advance in society by becoming revered and learned scholars or community leaders.

In modern times a new social hierarchy exists. The nobility and the wealthier families are still present, but the real elite in society are now the ethnic Chinese, who hold most of the better jobs in the administration.

Tibetan refugee children pose for a photo in Nepal.

REFUGEES

When the Dalai Lama fled Tibet in 1959, thousands of people followed and settled with him in India or moved to other countries, such as Nepal and Switzerland, as part of refugee settlement programs. Over the years the Chinese government has agreed to allow several delegations from the Dalai Lama into Tibet to carry out studies of the state of the people, but the Dalai Lama himself has never returned. Tibetans are free to return to Tibet, but on their entry visa they must state that they are Chinese citizens.

For many years the United States refused to accept Tibetans as political refugees, maintaining its policy of noninterference in China's domestic affairs. But more recently, Tibetans have been granted entrance into the United States. In 1993, one thousand displaced Tibetans living in India and Nepal landed on US soil, setting up small communities in cities such as New York and Minneapolis. The 2000 US Census reported 5,147 Tibetans living in the United States. A 2008 estimate put the number at around 9,000.

TRADITIONAL DRESS

The national dress of Tibet is the *chuba*, a long-sleeved loose cloak worn by both men and women. The cloak is wrapped around the body and fastened at the waist with a colorful belt. The blousy front of the chuba becomes the repository for everything from groceries to valuables. Underneath the chuba, a variety of shirts, vests, and jackets are worn to keep out the cold. Long woolen breeches are tucked into knee-high felt boots. Women wear long dresses and blouses, and an apron of brightly colored horizontal stripes.

A Tibetan woman in the Ngari Prefecture wears a colorful traditional outfit.

In the feudal past, a person's apparel was dictated by his or her social standing. Nomadic men wore a shorter version of the chuba made of sheepskin, and women wore a much longer version. Exact details of men's dress were laid down by decree. During the winter, from December to April, all lay and ecclesiastical officials had to wear fur hats and cloaks. After April no one could wear fur even if it was freezing!

Hats were once a very important feature of Tibetan dress. People were generally identified by the kinds of hats they wore, and as hats differed according to geographical region, a person from the south could be easily distinguished from a person from the north. Women's hats were often wooden frames that were covered in cloth and decorated with precious stones. The number and size of the stones on her hat indicated the extent of her wealth. These hats are still worn on special occasions today. Tibetan hats today are often made of fur and brocade and shaped like a flowerpot with flaps at the ears. The two most commonly seen men's hats in the towns are trilbies made from soft felt and homburgs.

Jewelry is an important element in both men's and women's dress in Tibet. Most women carry a prayer wheel, which they rotate as they walk. Over their clothes they wear silver amulets, coral and turquoise beads, prayer beads, and silver earrings and bracelets. Ladakhi women wear elaborate headdresses, covered in stones and turquoise beads, which extend down the length of their backs. Men often wear one earring and carry a tiny statue of a lama, a prayer wheel, or prayer beads.

INTERNET LINKS

www.migrationpolicy.org/article/global-nomads-emergence-tibetan-diaspora-part-i
This site gives a detailed explanation of the Tibetan diaspora around the world.

unpo.org/members/7879
The Unrepresented Nations and Peoples Organization offers an overview of Tibet and its people with links to relevant articles.

www.travelchinaguide.com/intro/nationality
This Chinese travel site lists links to all of the Chinese minority ethnic groups, including the Zang and others in the TAR.

www.tsechenkunchabling.com/tibetan-costume-fashion-from-roof-of-the-world
This site offers an in-depth overview of traditional Tibetan clothing, with many photos, including historical and regional variations.

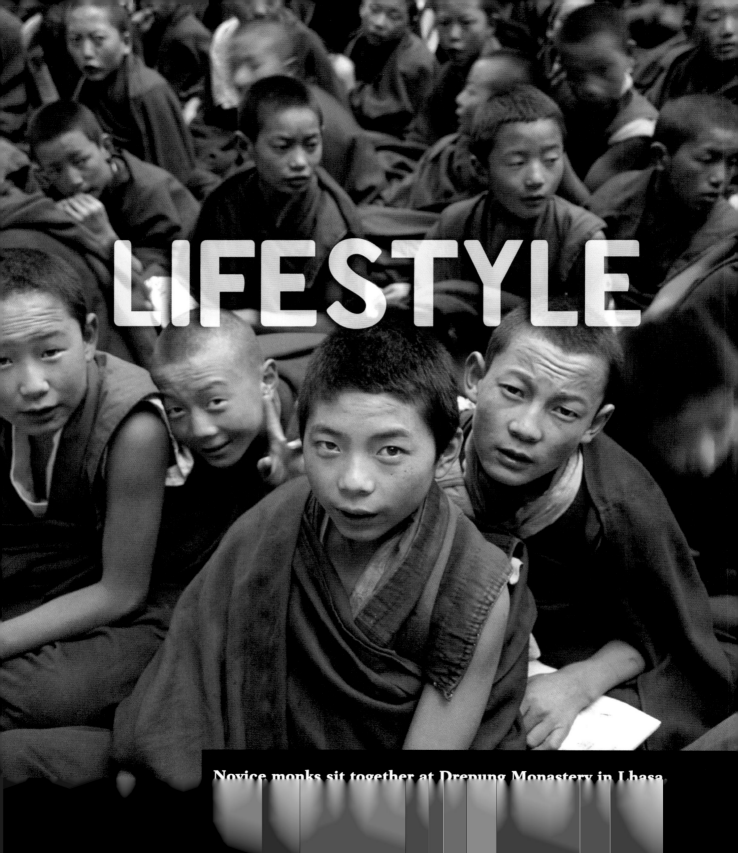

LIFESTYLE

Novice monks sit together at Drepung Monastery in Lhasa.

7

THE CHINESE INFLUENCE ON THE Tibetan lifestyle has been so strong that there is a word for it. The Sinicization or "Chinafication" of Tibet is seen by critics of the Chinese government as cultural assimilation or worse. China simply sees it as modernization. Either way, the lives of the Tibetan people have changed in many ways over the last sixty years. In the cities and towns, the Chinese influence is most strongly felt, in place of the traditional customs based on farming, bartering, and Buddhism. But as the Chinese administration relaxes its laws regarding religious worship, the number of Tibetans openly practicing Buddhism is increasing. The Chinese government hopes, however, that as the standard of living is raised, the Tibetan people will become less influenced by these religious beliefs.

In premodern Tibet, many families chose to have at least one son join a monastery. Such a move not only increased a family's social status but also benefited families living in poverty. Boys were sent into monastic training at a very young age, usually between the ages of six and twelve. In 1951, when China took over the country, an estimated 24 percent of all Tibetan males were celibate Buddhist monks.

CITY LIFE

Lhasa has a population of about five hundred thousand, with Chinese outnumbering Tibetans two to one. Most of the Chinese in the city work in civil service or are members of the military force. Local people are more likely to be engaged in trade, arts and crafts, and numerous other activities.

Many of the historic religious sites that were badly damaged during the Cultural Revolution are being restored at government expense; this project employs returned monks and craftsmen. During religious festivals people meet at the Jokhang Temple—the religious and cultural center of the old city. The temple is surrounded by a market composed of stores and street stalls set up by nomads and foreign and local traders.

In the new Chinese-built part of Lhasa, both Chinese and Tibetans live in work units—blocks of apartments in a walled compound with a large gateway. Tibetans in the old city live for the most part in whitewashed stone houses of two or three stories with black-framed windows that look out on narrow streets and are sheltered by elaborately carved, overhanging

eaves. People in both parts of the city now have access to electricity, indoor plumbing, and refuse facilities. In Lhasa, big, expensive department stores, where manufactured goods are sold, sit alongside traditional small shops selling local produce and handicrafts, giving shoppers a wide choice of goods.

Cattle stand outside a typical house in a rural Himalayan village.

LIFE IN THE COUNTRY

In the valleys of the south and southeast, villages may consist of one or two farmsteads, each supporting one family. The farmhouses are single-story, quadrangular buildings with an open courtyard inside. The entrance leads to the courtyard, which is encircled by the family's living quarters, storage rooms, barns, and pens for the animals. The flat roof is used for the storage of fuel (primarily yak dung and brushwood). Streams of flags fly around the house, each flag representing a prayer. As the wind blows, the prayer is repeated, bringing good fortune to the family. Farmland often stretches for several acres, depending on the size of the family. The variety of crops planted depends on the climate—barley, oats, apples, and pears in the areas with a harsher climate and wheat, apricots, and peaches in the warmer locations. Animals are very important in the village communities; there are very few communities where people do not spend part of their time with the herds in search of new pastures.

LIFE ON THE NORTHERN PLATEAU

The nomads live in the open plains of the Northern Plateau, traveling north in the summer and returning south in the winter. Their tents are made from yak fur that has been processed into thick waterproof felt by continuous soaking, drying, and beating. The tents are stretched over a wooden frame and held down with ropes. But most of the young people prefer to sleep outside in the open or among the flocks of sheep to keep warm.

Individual nomadic units are large, consisting of several families. They are very self-sufficient, only occasionally visiting settled areas to trade or to attend religious festivals. The nomads provide much of Tibet's meat in the form of sheep, lamb, and yak meat. They exchange the meat for tea, which is mostly imported from China, and *tsampa* (tsam-PA), the Tibetan staple made from roasted barley flour, tea, and butter.

A nomadic woman cooks yak milk inside her shelter.

The men spend most of their time away from the camp to tend the animals, while the women stay close to the tents. The work of making cloth, curing hides, spinning wool, cooking, and drying the meat for the winter are all carried out by the women. Men and women alike carry a slingshot that they often use to control wandering livestock or to fight off wild animals. They rarely hunt or eat wild animals, preferring their own domestic animals. Primitive rifles and throwing spears are other weapons used by the nomads. The men all carry large, elaborate, multipurpose knives.

MONASTERY LIFE

In the centuries before the arrival of the Chinese, thousands of boys (approximately one-fifth of the male population) and girls, as young as five and six years old, were sent to live in the monasteries. The nuns and monks all took a vow of celibacy along with many other renunciations, although it was quite customary for men and women to leave the order and marry, or to join after a period of married life.

Schooling began almost immediately after one's arrival at the monastery. Novices were tasked according to their aptitude, taking on different responsibilities in the monastery. Those who showed an intellectual disposition would continue to study, perhaps going on to become lamas, while others might become craftsmen or cooks, gardeners or policemen. The brighter students were educated for twenty-five years, periodically taking examinations in the form of debates with their teachers. For the nuns, though, there was little chance of intellectual advancement. Their roles were traditionally confined to the upkeep of the monastery.

Monasteries became important theological colleges, medical schools, and centers of art and culture. Running these businesses or owning the land was very profitable, as monasteries were free from taxation.

The Tibetan monasteries are currently being renovated, and becoming a monk is still a career path chosen by some Tibetans. Nevertheless, the numbers of monks and monasteries in Tibet are strictly regulated and children under the age of eighteen are forbidden from entering a religious order.

LIFE IN EXILE

Tibetans have been given refuge in many parts of the world, especially in the countries bordering Tibet, but the most important Tibetan community is at Dharamsala in India. Several thousand refugees fled to India with the Dalai Lama in 1959 and settled in a former hill station in the mountains. Over the years, temples, monasteries, schools, a medical college, the Institute for the Performing Arts, a library, and a museum dedicated to Tibetan culture have all been built to cater to the needs of the growing community of exiles.

The refugees are poor by Western standards; families often live in one room in a mud house with very basic or no indoor plumbing. They are employed in craft centers, producing traditional Tibetan carpets and jewelry, as well as T-shirts and bumper stickers with mottoes about Tibetan freedom. At the same time, these refugee communities are usually much better off than their immediate Indian or Nepalese neighbors.

There are more than thirty-six Tibetan refugee colonies scattered around other areas in India and Nepal. Most of these communities rely primarily on agriculture, but many have developed flourishing carpet industries, in some cases running large export businesses. Tibetan refugees are gradually absorbing the culture of their adopted countries. Children find it necessary to learn local languages rather than Tibetan in order to pass their exams. There is now a third generation of refugees who have never lived in Tibet, and as time passes it is becoming less and less likely that they will ever return to their homeland.

A Tibetan refugee works in a weaving house in Kathmandu, Nepal.

ROLE OF WOMEN

For centuries Tibetan society was a highly mobile one. As a result, men and women were often separated for months at a time, the men going off with their herds and the women remaining at the camp or village to look after their crops and their families. Consequently, women spent part of the year in charge of the household and became very independent, both economically and socially. Still, positions of power in the community and in business were held by men, and only men could become lamas. The Dalai Lama's government, local administrators, and village chieftains were traditionally positions filled by men.

A wife was responsible for running the household, negotiating with traders, and controlling the family finances. She often owned property that she could count on keeping even if her husband divorced her. Today, young Tibetan women are more likely to identify with their Chinese counterparts than their own mothers, particularly in areas like Lhasa where the Chinese have a strong influence. Schoolchildren are taught to conform to Chinese ideals of gender roles, dress, and marriage, which are very different from those of traditional Tibet. For many years, any kind of adornment, including braided hair, was frowned on and in some cases forbidden, despite its social and religious importance to the Tibetans. Marriages are controlled by the work unit, which grants licenses based on government criteria. Tibetan women are limited to two children and one husband only. Application to the work unit must also be made in order for a woman to travel, to bear a child, or to study. Women now have the right to hold office, but few Tibetans, either women or men, hold positions in the bureaucracy, which is dominated by the ethnic Chinese.

MARRIAGE

The planning for a traditional Tibetan wedding begins with choosing an auspicious day for the event. When the day finally arrives, the groom's family sends for the bride, who must appear unwilling to go with them. She is accompanied by members of her family, but no one who has been recently bereaved may accompany her. The bride will have to refuse to enter into the house of the groom until she is offered a pail of yak milk by her future mother-in-law. When the ceremony is over, the parents and the bride and groom receive visitors at the groom's house. They wear traditional silk chubas made especially for this special day, greeting the guests as they file in. Each guest brings six silk scarves, which are presented to the groom's parents and the bride and groom. Red paper packets containing money are also common gifts. Yak dung, the main fuel of the Tibetans, and a pail of water decorated with butter are kept outside the door, symbolizing fertility.

Once the formalities are complete, the party begins and can last up to six days. Meals are served at regular intervals and Tibetan beer is drunk. For the Tibetan Chinese, arranged marriages, subject to parental consent, are very common. Country girls often take older city husbands in order to get a permit to live in the city.

HAVING A FAMILY

The policy limiting how many children a couple can have is relaxed for the "ethnic minorities," as the Chinese call groups like the Tibetans, and for Chinese people settling in Tibet. However, those having any more than two children are penalized: the third and consecutive children get no food ration until they are eighteen, and no free medical care or education. Since Tibetans are mostly poor, this can be a serious consideration.

Since the Chinese lifted the ban on religious practice, newborn babies are once again taken to the lama to be named in a traditional name-giving ceremony. During the times when there were no lamas or monks to carry out these duties, no one knew how to name their children and so children acquired some peculiar names. Many were named in the order of their place in the family. Others were named after the day of the week on which they were born. Others were given ugly names in the hope that it would keep any malevolent ancestral spirits from claiming the child before its time.

DEATH RITUALS

Tibetan Buddhists believe that death signifies the departure of the soul from the body, rendering the body a lifeless shell. If the soul has not reached a state of enlightenment, it will be reincarnated in a new body. It is important that Tibetans contribute to the cycle of life and rebirth in order to give back the lives that they have taken—to kill any living thing even for food is a sin. Sky burial is a funeral rite that allows Tibetans to make atonement. In a sky burial, the body is carried up to a place high in the mountains where it is cut up into pieces and left for the eagles and vultures. In this way the body provides food for a soul undergoing another incarnation on earth. Skilled men are hired to do this job, as no one wants a relative's body to be left uneaten. Tibetans believe that it is inauspicious for carrion birds not to eat the remains in a sky burial. They believe that when that happens it is a sign from the heavens that something bad is about to take place.

Since the opening of Tibet's borders, there are reports that some tourists have watched the sky burials, angering many Tibetans for whom this ritual is considered sacred. Recently, tourists have been banned from the sites, although some unscrupulous tour operators are planning to set up viewing platforms with telescopes on neighboring peaks.

Another common burial ceremony, reserved primarily for paupers and children, is river burial, where the body is carried to a river so that it might provide food for fish. Fishing in these sacred rivers, as some Chinese people like to do, is a double insult both to the soul that is incarnated as the fish, and to the body of the person it has eaten.

When highly regarded Tibetans, such as lamas, pass away, they are cremated. In some cases the cremated remains are divided and sent to various monasteries to be interred in stupas or mausoleums. Burial in the hard, rocky ground is very rare in Tibet with the exception of the Lhobas, a group of pastoral Tibetans living in southeast Tibet, who bury their dead in the ground.

EDUCATION

Before the arrival of the Chinese there was no universal education in Tibet. Most formal education took place either in the monasteries or under the guidance of private tutors, as in the case of the nobility. Illiteracy was perhaps 90 percent.

Today, education is free and compulsory at the primary and secondary levels. In 2010, the enrollment of children in public school was about 98.8 percent. In the more heavily populated areas where there are many Chinese settlers, Tibetan and Chinese children attend different primary

The twelve Tibetan students of Xiangnong primary school in the TAR learn from the only teacher in the village.

schools and are taught in their mother tongues with a few hours of instruction in other languages each week.

A public examination for places in middle school is taken by Tibetans at the age of twelve. A pass in the Chinese language is essential in order to obtain a place because classes are taught in Chinese. Tibet University opened in 1985, with two campuses, and has been expanded in recent years with the addition of an art school, medical college, economic college, and other specialty colleges. The College of Tibetan Medicine launched postgraduate programs in 1998; the first class graduated in 2002. Today, the university has about 7,500 students with ethnic Tibetans forming 67 percent of the student body. The Department of Tibetan Studies attracts students from around the world.

MEDICINE

As late as the 1950s, Tibetan medicine was as much an aspect of religion as it was science. Heinrich Harrer, an Austrian writer who lived in Tibet for seven years at a time when it was closed to Westerners, reported that he did not observe any surgical procedure being performed during his long stay in the territory. Illnesses in Tibet were treated as matters of the spirit rather than of the body. Before the eighth century a form of surgery was practiced in Tibet, but it was banned after the Chinese emperor's mother died during a surgical operation.

Traditional Tibetan medicine is based on the belief of there being three humors in the body—wind, bile, and phlegm—rather like the medieval European medical theory. The Tibetan doctor relies heavily on reading the pulse of the patient and analyzing his or her urine to determine whether there is too much or too little of each one of the humors. Astrology plays an important role in curing the sick as well. The doctor takes careful note of the stars dominating the patient's birth and those dominating at the time of illness before making a diagnosis. Once a diagnosis has been made, the illness is treated with wild herbs that are collected and dried by monks. Acupuncture (inserting needles into bodily tissues at particular points) is also used in the treatment of ailments. Like the Chinese, Tibetans believe that a life essence flows through the body, keeping the bodily functions in balance. Illness can be brought on if the life essence is prevented from running its normal course. Acupuncture, acupressure, and moxibustion (a form of heat treatment) are used to restore the healthy flow.

When the Dalai Lama fled in 1959, many skilled Tibetan doctors went with him, and a medical school, the Men-Tsee-Khang, or Tibetan Medical and Astrological Institute, was soon established in Dharamsala. Today, it employs doctors, astrologers, and nearly three hundred staff members, and has fifty-one branch medical clinics in India. Tibetan herbal cures are a major export of the exiled community.

INTERNET LINKS

freedomhouse.org/report/freedom-world/2016/tibet
This organization assesses the civil liberties of the Tibetan people.

www.men-tsee-khang.org/index2.htm
This is the site of the Tibetan Medical and Astrological Institute in Dharamsala, India.

www.takingcharge.csh.umn.edu/explore-healing-practices/tibetan-medicine
This quick overview by the University of Minnesota gives a good introduction to Tibetan medicine.

news.xinhuanet.com/english/2016-05/06/c_135340086.htm
Colorful photos of a Tibetan wedding ceremony are featured on this site.

RELIGION

The Dalai Lama speaks on the subject of kindness at a US Conference of Mayors meeting in June 2016.

9

BUDDHISM CAME TO TIBET FROM India and China in stages, replacing an earlier animistic and shamanistic religion called Bön. The Buddhist faith is such an integral part of Tibetan life that Tibet has become almost synonymous with the faith. Although the majority of Tibetans are Buddhist, there is also a small deep-rooted Muslim community in Tibet. For many years all religion was banned in China. But in today's more liberal climate, some ethnic Chinese in Tibet and in greater China are rediscovering their spiritual heritage.

The Chinese authorities have had difficulty dampening popular reverence for the Dalai Lama in Tibet. In June 2015, despite an official ban and threats of arrest, many Tibetans celebrated the Dalai Lama's eightieth birthday in both public and private.

THE BÖN RELIGION

Bön existed before any form of writing emerged in Tibet, so its origins are unknown. The word Bön is the Tibetan name for "Tibet," and although the Bön religion still exists, it is now very different from its early forms. In its earliest stages, the Bön religion was a simple form of animism (the belief that all things, animate or inanimate, possess a spirit); it was a means by which believers thought they could be protected from hostile spiritual forces. Ancestral and celestial spirits and the natural elements had to be appeased through magical rites. Bön followers also believed that shamans (people thought to have a direct connection to the spirit world) could protect them from these spirits. With the arrival of Buddhism in Tibet, the Buddhist canon soon posed a theological challenge to the established religion. The Bön religion thus evolved, taking on new complexities.

BUDDHISM

Tibetan Buddhism differs from other forms of Buddhism in that it has acquired some elements of the shamanism and magic of Bön. Like all other Buddhists, Tibetan Buddhists believe that existence is filled with suffering and anguish. In order to escape this kind of suffering, called *duhkha*, a state of enlightenment and transcendence called nirvana is sought where the believer is freed from the pain and suffering of the world. For Tibetan Buddhists, there are three ways to achieve enlightenment: the lesser path, or Hinayana; the greater path, or Mahayana; and the diamond path, or Tantrayana.

HINAYANA This is the way of life adopted by the majority of people in Tibet. The ordinary route to enlightenment is based on a personal commitment to achieve nirvana for the individual's own sake. To achieve a state of nirvana, Buddhists often follow a prescribed school of thought, or path: for some it is Hinayana or "the lesser path."

On this path one must make a commitment to the Three Jewels—the Buddha, the dharma, and the sangha. This means that a Buddhist's life should be dedicated to enlightenment, symbolized by the Buddha himself, and adherence to the dharma, a set of laws established by Buddha. The sangha is a community of people committed to enlightenment such as a Buddhist religious community or monastery.

In childhood, Tibetan Buddhists make a commitment to the Three Jewels in the presence of a lama. They repeat this commitment regularly throughout their lives, rather in the way that some Christian children are brought into the church at the age of seven and then confirmed in their belief when they turn thirteen.

MAHAYANA Followers of this path seek to achieve the highest stage of nirvana not only for themselves, but also for the sake of all living things. Their goal is to become a bodhisattva. The bodhisattva refrains from entering nirvana in order to guide others on the path to enlightenment. They must show generosity, ethics, tolerance, energy, and wisdom. Bodhisattvas have cleared their minds of all desire and can see the world as it really is. After reaching this state, they help other people achieve the same state.

Compassion for others, epitomized by the life of a bodhisattva, is central to Tibetan Buddhism. It can be heard in the repeated prayer *om mani padme hum* (OM-MAN-ee-PAD-may-HUM). Prior to the Chinese invasion, the walls and hillsides of Tibet were covered with the words of this prayer. The prayer *om mani padme hum* is roughly translated as follows: *om* (the sound that symbolizes the body, speech and mind of Buddha), *mani* (jewel), *padme* (lotus), *hum* (so be it). Jewel in the Lotus is one of the many names for the Buddha.

TANTRAYANA Similar to Mahayanists, followers of this tradition seek personal enlightenment to show compassion for others. But this path to enlightenment is more complex. Each stage of enlightenment on this path is represented by a deity. As Tantrayanists move to the next stage, they call on the god representing that stage to help them. Using yoga, Tantrayanists channel their energy toward the essence of this god.

Tibetan temples were once covered in paintings depicting these deities, some of them calm and benign, others fierce and angry, all of them representing aspects of this path to enlightenment. Through meditation and yoga, practitioners believe they will eventually see a special clear light that ordinary people can only see in the few hours before death.

BARDO Buddhists believe that the soul has no beginning. It has always existed and goes on being reborn into new bodies until it finally reaches a state of enlightenment. This process is called reincarnation. After death, the soul passes through the state of bardo. It is here that those who have achieved enlightenment can see the clear light indicating their ascent to nirvana. Nirvana is the state when the soul has finally been released from the endless cycle of death and rebirth, called *samsara*. Bardo consists of seven

Intricately decorated prayer wheels are for sale in Lhasa.

stages, each subdivided into seven more, so that the soul has forty-nine days in which to wander in bardo seeking the clear light. At some stage during those forty-nine days, the unenlightened will be drawn back into the world and reincarnated as another living being.

DAILY WORSHIP

After 1959, all displays of religious faith were prohibited in Tibet. It was not until the 1980s that religious persecution began to ease. Though they were apprehensive at first, more and more people began to return to their old ways of worship. Every home once had its own shrine, and these began to reappear with photographs of the Dalai Lama as the centerpiece.

Prayer wheels also began to reappear. Before the Chinese invasion, these handheld prayer wheels would have been carried by almost everyone. A much larger version of the prayer wheel could also be found at the temples.

Devotees would spin rows of these huge prayer wheels in a clockwise direction as they entered the temple. The wheels had scriptures inscribed on them and devotees believed spinning them had the same effect as chanting the mantras out loud. These wheels are now being restored.

Tibetans are beginning once again to make pilgrimages to sacred sites. Some people make their way to these holy places entirely through a series of small steps followed by prostrations. A few pilgrims actually travel hundreds of miles in this way. The pilgrims and worshippers bring gifts of incense and flowers, or butter to fuel the lamps in the temple. Some people offer seven bowls of clean water symbolizing the seven limbs of prayer. The seven aspects include prostrating, offering, and confession.

With the revival in religion, superstition is returning to Tibet as well. Some Tibetans believe that ailments can be cured by rubbing parts of their bodies on holy relics, while others hope that their intelligence will be sharpened by placing pins on religious statues.

A Buddhist devotee spins the row of prayer wheels upon entering a temple.

THE WHEEL OF LIFE

Complex diagrams of the Wheel of Life are often drawn on the walls of Tibetan Buddhist temples. The wheel shows the universe without beginning or end and the countless world systems that exist within this universe. Within each world system there are six basic forms of life: humans, animals, deities, titans, ghosts, and denizens of hell.

The pig, snake, and rooster at the hub of the wheel represent ignorance, hatred, and desire, respectively. These are the things that keep the spirit trapped in the Wheel of Life. The individual spirit has no beginning in the Wheel of Life; it has always existed and has been reborn many times over. The way in which the spirit has conducted itself in one incarnation determines its destiny in the next life. The next circle shows the spirits of those who have almost achieved enlightenment but have been thrown back down into hell because of a lack of will. The six realms of existence into which the spirit is continually reborn are depicted in the next ring, while the outermost ring shows the twelve stages of mortal life, from ignorance in the previous life to aging and death in the next.

All of the images in the intricate Wheel of Life have symbolic meaning.

THE PANCHEN LAMA

The Panchen Lama is second only to the Dalai Lama in religious authority for the Gelugpa school of Tibetan Buddhism. The first incarnation of the Panchen Lama was born in the fourteenth century; his reincarnations continued unhindered until the death of the ninth lama in 1937. It was not until 1950, thirteen years after his death, that two Tibetan candidates were discovered. Relations between the Chinese and the Tibetans had been deteriorating, so when the Chinese put forward a candidate, the Tibetans feared the political situation would worsen if he were turned down. Despite the fact that traditional tests were not administered, the Chinese candidate gradually came to be accepted as the true incarnation. He was taken to Beijing at the age of fourteen, where his training and education were strictly controlled by the Chinese government.

After the Dalai Lama fled Tibet in 1959, the Panchen Lama was declared the political and spiritual leader of Tibet. When he was allowed to return to Tibet, he declared his allegiance to the Dalai Lama and was subsequently arrested. He spent years in Chinese prisons and was only pardoned in the late 1970s. His death in 1989 sparked a search for his incarnation. In 1995, the Dalai Lama announced the discovery of a six-year-old Panchen Lama.

The Chinese authorities took the boy into their custody and nobody except the Chinese government knows of his whereabouts today. Not long afterward, the Chinese conferred the title of Panchen Lama on their own candidate, Gyaltsen Norbu. The dispute over the disappearance of the missing Panchen Lama (pictured in protest posters, right), as well as the legitimacy of the Chinese candidate, remains unresolved.

LAMAS

Lama means "teacher." A lama, like a bodhisattva, is someone who has achieved a state of enlightenment and becomes a spiritual teacher to help others along the same path. Lamas are important because as the student seeking enlightenment advances to each higher level, he needs to be assisted by someone who can show him the nature of the next stage.

Most Tibetan monasteries have one or two holy men who are believed to have chosen not to achieve nirvana but to be reincarnated so that they may help more people to a state of enlightenment. The two most important lamas in Tibet are the Dalai Lama and the Panchen Lama.

FINDING THE INCARNATIONS

Discovering the rebirth of a lama is not an easy affair. Unusual remarks made by a lama prior to his death are duly noted as possible clues to the location of his rebirth, but it could be days or years before the child-incarnate is found.

When the thirteenth Dalai Lama died, there were no clear indications as to where the incarnate could be found, so the lamas waited for a sign. As the embalmed body of the thirteenth Dalai Lama lay in state, his head began to turn in one direction. This sent the searchers to a lake reputed to be an oracle. After meditating near the lake the lamas experienced a vision of a green roofed building near a temple. When they finally located the building in their vision in northeast Tibet, they found a child of two there who purportedly recognized one of the Dalai Lama's followers and who claimed some of the thirteenth Dalai Lama's personal possessions as his own. The child, the present Dalai Lama, was immediately moved to the monastery in Lhasa where he lived until his exile in 1959.

THE SEARCH FOR THE TRUE KARMAPA

Tibetan Buddhism is divided into several sects, distinguished by the color of the hats they wear. The members of one sect, the black hats or the Kagyu, are still arguing over the identity of its seventeenth leader. Leaders of the Kagyu sect are titled Karmapa Lama.

In 1992 the son of a Tibetan nomad, whose birth had been accompanied by wondrous signs, was found. The child, named Ugyen Trinley Dorje, was enthroned at a monastery in Lhasa with the Dalai Lama's approval (he too had seen visions confirming the identity of the child). But in 1994, a second child turned up in the protection of a former regent of the lama. Of Tibetan origin, and two years older than Ugyen Trinley Dorje, this child is said to have revealed his "true identity" to his parents when he was just three years old.

The adherents of the two reincarnations accuse each other of being agents of the Chinese who, they say, are seeking to get their hands on the wealth of the Kagyu sect. In 2000, Karmapa Ugyen Trinley Dorje fled Tibet and now resides near the Dalai Lama's exiled community in Dharamsala, India.

RELIGIOUS SYMBOLS

The seventeenth Karmapa, Ugyen Trinley Dorje, leads a prayer in New Delhi.

Hung from the roofs of buildings, trees, and poles, prayer flags are the most prevalent religious symbol in Tibet. As the wind blows, the prayer printed on the flag is released, bringing luck and prosperity to religious devotees.

The swastika is a common symbol of both Tibetan Buddhism and the Bön religion. Drawn clockwise, the swastika is the Buddhist symbol of good fortune. Drawn counterclockwise it represents the Bön symbol of good fortune.

The bell and *dorje* (DOOR-jay), a stick used to chime bells, form another ubiquitous religious symbol. The dorje symbolizes a thunderbolt and the bell's chime is said to drive away evil spirits.

The lotus flower is featured in many Tibetan Buddhist paintings and murals because it symbolizes nirvana, the state of complete enlightenment. A representation of two fish, often painted on the walls of houses, symbolizes the souls of people liberated by religious faith.

THE SACRED MANDALA

The Buddhist cosmos is often depicted in mandalas, which are complex patterns of squares and circles in perfect radial symmetry. They can be created in paint and three-dimensional architecture but are often formed with grains of colored sand, an ancient art form. Tibetan Buddhist monks use mandalas to aid meditation.

The word mandala *comes from Sanskrit, meaning "circle." Designs based on radial symmetry—which is symmetry around a central axis—are important in both Hinduism and Buddhism, but also appear in Christian art, such as in stained-glass rose windows in cathedrals. A Tibetan Buddhist mandala is more than just a design, however. Everything about the sacred mandala—its colors, patterns, and imagery—is symbolic of a perfectly harmonious universe and exhibits the wisdom of enlightenment.*

Monks skilled in making mandalas sometimes spend weeks creating one out of sand on a tabletop or on the ground outside a monastery. Creating a sand mandala is said to aid purification and healing on several levels. Typically, a mandala is divided into four quadrants and four monks work together, each on his own quadrant. The creation begins with a ceremony of music and chanting. The artists then draw the design using white chalk, a straight-edged ruler, and a compass. The process can take about three hours. At that point, the artists begin in the center and work outward, using colored sands poured through a narrow funnel-shaped tool called a chakpur.

One of the important aspects of a sand mandala is its impermanence, which is, itself, a central tenet of Buddhism. After spending weeks, perhaps, making a magnificent and intricate work of art, the creator destroys it by brushing all the sand together. Traditionally, the sands are then spilled into a stream to spread the blessings of the mandala. The deconstruction is a fitting demonstration of the impermanence of all things.

Pilgrims on long journeys can often be seen carrying mani stones. These small stones have the prayer *om mani padme hum* carved or painted on them. When they reach the temple or holy place, pilgrims lay the stones in huge piles outside the entrance.

Sculpted butter and tsampa are considered sanctified food and are presented to the temples during festivals. These sculptures are often intricately carved out of blocks of colored butter and are products of many hours of hard work.

A collection of mani stones are displayed at the Chiu Gompa Monastery in Tibet.

INTERNET LINKS

www.bbc.co.uk/religion/religions/buddhism
This is the entry page to the extensive BBC Religion section on Buddhism.

www.buddhanet.net/e-learning/buddhistworld/tibet-txt.htm
This overview includes links to a timeline and an article on Tibetan Buddhist art.

www.dalailama.com/messages/buddhism
The official site of the Dalai Lama addresses many aspects of Tibetan Buddhism.

www.religionfacts.com/tibetan-buddhism
This site gives a good introduction to Tibetan Buddhism and its history.

www.yowangdu.com/tibetan-buddhism/sand-mandalas.html
This site offers a good explanation of the sand mandala with photos and a video.

LANGUAGE

A young Tibetan monk studies an ancient Buddhist manuscript in a monastery in 2013.

LANGUAGE IS A DIRECT REFLECTION of history. Tibet's centuries of physical isolation manifests in the language—Tibetan, unlike many other tongues, is relatively free of foreign influences. Tibetan belongs to a very large family of languages known as Tibeto-Burmese, which falls within an even larger family of languages known as Sino-Tibetan. Its offshoots are spoken in the TAR, large areas of Sichuan, Yunnan, Gansu, and Qinghai provinces in China, and parts of Sikkim, Ladakh, and Nepal. Although there are several dialects of Tibetan spoken in and around Tibet, they are all mutually intelligible.

Since the arrival of the Chinese, Tibetan has become a second language for younger students. At higher levels, Chinese is the language of instruction. English was never widely spoken in Tibet and is unknown outside urban areas. As the need for international communication increases, many Tibetans are beginning to see English as a means of bettering their lives; therefore, a few English-language schools are now in operation.

Beginning in 2012, China reportedly scaled back sharply on the teaching of Tibetan and other native languages of the ethnic minorities in the western regions. Many supposedly bilingual public schools were ordered to switch to offering instruction primarily in Chinese, even at the elementary level, so as to "make sure minority students master and use the basic common language."

WRITING

There are four different ways of writing the thirty consonants and four vowels of the Tibetan alphabet, depending on the occasion. The most stylized—the equivalent of English capital letters—is called *U-chen* (you-CHEN) and is used in printed text and inscriptions, as well as in a large number of handwritten texts. *U-me* (you-MAY) is more flowing and ornate and is used in the vast majority of handwritten texts, letters, and archival documents. The two other scripts are simpler and are used in everyday writing. If two words have the same sound but different meanings, which is common, one will be written with an extra consonant to indicate the difference.

SPOKEN TIBETAN

Spoken Tibetan is more similar to European languages than to Chinese because it is phonetic, meaning that the alphabet represents the sounds of the letters rather than the actual meaning of the word. Most Tibetan words have only one or two syllables, but prefixes and suffixes can be added to alter its pronunciation or meaning. At one time spoken Tibetan had multiple consonant clusters that would have made it very difficult for English speakers to pronounce, but in modern Tibetan these have largely disappeared.

The word order of a Tibetan sentence is always subject/object/verb. In Tibetan, there are no words that are equivalent to "yes" or "no." Instead the final part of the verb is repeated either affirmatively or negatively. There are three basic tenses in Tibetan that correspond to the English past, present, and future tenses. Each verb consists of two words, the first indicating the meaning and the second showing the tense, so that *nyo ge ray* (neo-ge-RAY) means "buying" or "going to buy," while *nyo song* (neo-SONG) means "bought."

MANTRAS

Mantras are special forms of language that have a ritualistic or magical quality. Written in Sanskrit, they are ancient prayers thought to be able to precipitate and condense energies. They generally begin and end with two very special sounds: *om*, which is considered the "seed sound," the origin and essence of all life; and *hum*, which focuses the energies of the person who is chanting. Uttered correctly, the sound om is thought to put the individual in tune with all the voices of the world, all the sounds of nature, and the cosmos. People spend a lifetime learning to iterate the sound correctly.

The most common Tibetan mantra is *om mani padme hum*. It refers to the Buddha and translates as "Jewel in the Lotus." This mantra is often written on

A stone engraved with Tibetan script spells out the Buddhist mantra *"om mani padme hum."*

stones outside the monasteries, printed on prayer flags and prayer wheels, or written on tiny pieces of paper and worn in lockets to protect the wearer.

Another of the oldest Buddhist mantras is *om gate gate paragate parasamgate bodhi svaha*. It means "Gone, gone, completely gone, totally crossed over beyond the farthest shore. So be it."

CHINESE

Chinese is a very different language from Tibetan. It has eight major dialects, none of them mutually intelligible, so that spoken Mandarin is as foreign to a Cantonese speaker as English. But all the Chinese dialects are expressed in the same written form, so people can communicate by the written word throughout China, and the news in the daily newspapers is understood by all.

Written Chinese is based on a series of pictograms that once were actual drawings of the things they represent. It is still possible to see, for example, the shape of a man in the character that represents man. Some Chinese characters are very simple, requiring only one or two brushstrokes, but others take up to twenty strokes to complete. For children, learning to write in Chinese can be very difficult. Each character has to be memorized, unlike in English where a child, upon hearing a new word, can probably guess its spelling from its pronunciation.

Mandarin, the official language of China, has about four hundred syllables. Each syllable has four different vocal tones—each tone giving the character a different meaning. For example, the syllable *ma* can mean "mother," "hemp," "horse," or "to scold," depending on the tone in which it is said.

Getting a job in the civil service or in any industry that involves dealing with the public in Tibet is dependent upon whether one knows how to speak in Mandarin. In fact, it is becoming more and more usual to hear Tibetans in Lhasa speaking to one another in Mandarin.

BOOKS AND PRINTING

Books were originally printed in Tibet for the sole purpose of propagating Buddhist doctrine. Traditionally, the monasteries produced all printed materials in Tibet. Printing was a very laborious task. First the text was copied onto a sheet of paper. The page of writing was stuck face down on a wooden block, leaving an ink impression of the text in reverse on the surface of the block. The paper was then removed and the letters were carved out following the ink image. When the carving was complete, the surface of the carved block was oiled to strengthen it. When more copies of the text were needed, the

An artisan carves a wooden block for printing.

blocks would have to be taken out, used, and then stored again. Each monastery had large rooms containing thousands of blocks. Only one copy could be made at a time, and individuals were asked to bring their own inks and paper to the monastery.

Traditionally, books were not bound. Each bundle of loose sheets was held together with wooden binding boards, often intricately carved and studded with precious stones, and then wrapped in cloth.

To Tibetans, books are more than just repositories of knowledge. Like mantras, they embody the wisdom or faith or doctrine that they contain. When whole libraries of books were burned and their precious bindings stolen during the Cultural Revolution, the Tibetans considered this more than just an act of theft and vandalism. It was seen as a desecration of their faith.

THE MEDIA

All media in Tibet is strictly controlled by the Chinese government. Newspapers, radio programs, television shows, and films reflect the position of the Chinese Communist Party. Tibetans have virtually no access to independent news sources, and indeed, foreign journalists and media outlets are not allowed into the region. Broadband internet was introduced in 2003 in Lhasa, but even in this new media, the Chinese authorities maintain vigilant supervision and broad censorship.

All of these restrictions on the media are justified in the name of stability, according to a Tibet-specific policy called "the Four Stabilities" that the government introduced in 2012. The main objective is to prevent separatist voices from reaching an audience, and most particularly, to squash any communication from or about the Dalai Lama.

INTERNET LINKS

www.hrw.org/news/2012/07/13/china-attempts-seal-tibet-outside-information
Human Rights Watch details the Chinese government's crackdown on Tibetan media.

www.omniglot.com/writing/tibetan.htm
Omniglot offers a basic introduction to the Tibetan written language and useful phrases.

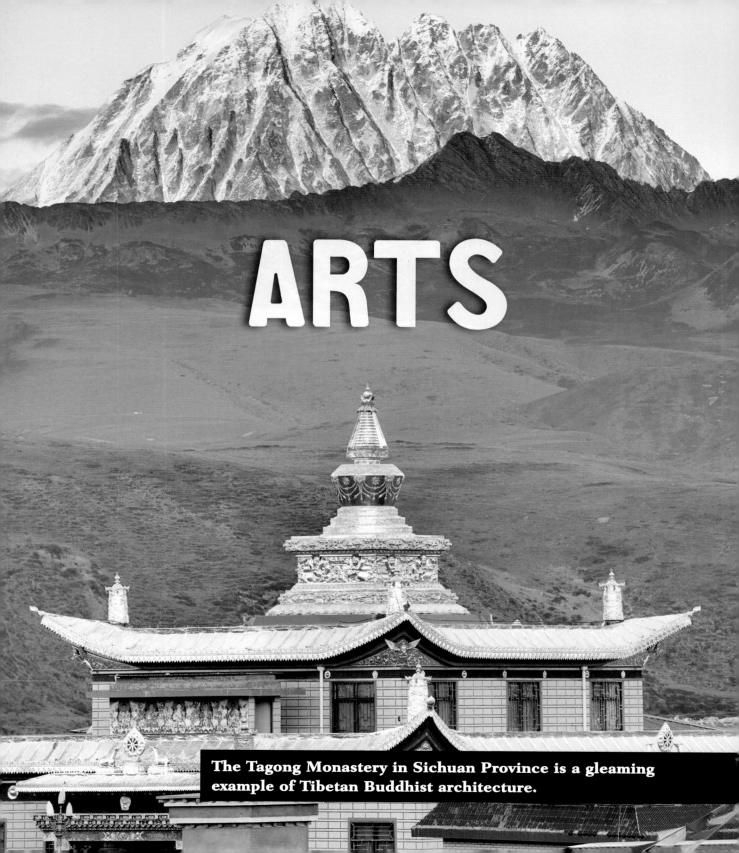

ARTS

The Tagong Monastery in Sichuan Province is a gleaming example of Tibetan Buddhist architecture.

10

THE STORY OF TIBETAN ART IS essentially the story of Buddhist art, for they are largely one and the same. In this culture, art is a manifestation of religion, not an expression of individual creativity; therefore, the making of the various art forms follows strict rules for proportion, color, imagery, and design.

Paintings are traditionally confined to mandalas, murals on temple walls, and huge banners called *thangkas* (THANG-kas) that are hung outside the monasteries during religious festivals. Music is dedicated to prayer chants and hymns. Literature is largely religious in nature, although some older folk tales have survived from the oral traditions that predate the arrival of Buddhism. Even traditional Tibetan theater takes the form of dance-dramas depicting stories from the Buddhist scriptures. The grandest architectural endeavors in Tibet are monasteries and temples, and even handicrafts such as jewelry—consisting primarily of amulets or ornaments—and carpets usually have religious significance.

Tibet's greatest architectural works are its monasteries and temples, which take the form of whole cities built within towering walls. They are often built around a central courtyard and contain prayer halls, libraries, dormitories, printing presses, kitchens, and stables. The focal point of every temple is the *chorten*, a shrine that often holds the remains of a revered lama.

THANGKAS

Thangkas are painted banners of linen, wool, or silk. The cloth is stretched out on a frame and coated with a paste made from talcum powder and animal glue; this blocks the pores of the cloth. When the material has dried, the outline of the painting is drawn on with charcoal sticks, sometimes from a paper template. Thangkas are considered sacred artifacts, and the painting is done on astrologically favorable days. Often the artist is assisted by a whole team of laypeople and monks whose job it is to make sure that the painting conforms to the strict rules set down for thangka painting. Upon its completion—a process that can take many years—it is sent to the lama who commissioned it. His hand- or footprint is then used as a mark of consecration.

Paints are made from minerals such as cinnabar, malachite, or plant dyes mixed with animal glue and ox bile, which gives them a luster. A brocade or silk border is added to the finished painting, and rollers are attached at the top and bottom so that it can be displayed. Thangkas are usually rectangular or square and depict Buddhas, deities, or the lives of the saints. Very few thangkas portray the daily lives of Tibetans. Thangkas are stored in monasteries and displayed during religious festivals.

The hanging of the thangkas before a ritual festival is a very important ceremony. Some of them are so big that dozens of monks are required just to haul them out of the storeroom. Like all Tibetan art, the production of thangkas is revered as an act of worship.

WOOD CARVING AND SCULPTURE

Tibetan wood carving is another example of the dedicated artistry that goes into the decoration of Tibetan temples. Any wooden part of a Tibetan temple is a possible site for wood carvings. Wooden Buddha statues and painted wooden tablets with designs similar to the thangkas are also common. Even small shrines in people's houses might be elaborately carved or painted.

A wooden statue portrays Buddha in meditation.

Stone carvings are also a very popular art form in Tibet. The majority of carvings are of a religious nature, such as representations of Buddhist deities, although it is common to see carved stone lions standing guard at the entrance to many of Tibet's buildings.

Carvings on mountain cliffs or rock faces line the routes that pilgrims take on their way to a monastery or some other religious site. These are often very simply carved with the figure of the Buddha or inscribed with scriptures or mantras. Pilgrims often prostrate themselves before the carvings in the belief that their travel weariness will be relieved by the act of prayer. Some of these ancient carvings were vandalized during the Cultural Revolution; but many are being painstakingly restored and rebuilt.

TIBETAN FRESCOES

These paintings cover the interior walls of monasteries and temples all over Tibet. Although the Cultural Revolution caused much damage to many beautiful examples of this ancient art form, some of them have fortunately been either left unscathed or are at least restorable.

In the seventeenth century two schools of art developed in Tibet: the Mentang and the Qenze schools. Both philosophies laid down strict rules about the materials to be used, the proportions of the figures, and the content of the background details. The Buddha figures were to reflect serenity and had to be drawn in single lines with even coloring. The backgrounds were to be painted as if viewed from above, and designs were geometric. These brightly colored frescoes depicted a wide range of subjects, ranging from the lives of ordinary Tibetans to scenes from the life of Buddha or images of deities.

BRONZE

Tibetans have been mining and crafting metals such as gold, silver, copper, and iron for thousands of years. They picked up these skills from artisans from India, Nepal, and China. Like the monastery frescoes, the creation of Buddhist bronzes was governed by rigid artistic rules. The specifications for a religious statue were often described in such careful detail that two images of the same deity were likely to be nearly identical. Surviving bronzes vary in size from huge statues of the Buddha weighing several tons to tiny ones small enough to be carried on the person.

LITERATURE, FOLKLORE, MYTHS, AND LEGENDS

The most important of Tibet's sacred literary works is the 108-volume *Kanjur*, the translation of the Buddha's words. Similar to the Christian Bible, it is by these words that many Tibetans live their lives. The *Tenjur* is another important text. Consisting of 225 volumes, it is a translation of commentaries on religious ideas and hymns. There is also the book known to the West as

MILAREPA

Born in 1040 to a family of middle-ranking nobles, Milarepa had every prospect of becoming a wealthy nobleman. But when his father died, the estate passed into his uncle's hands until Milarepa came of age. The unscrupulous uncle took the estate for himself and forced Milarepa's mother, brothers, and sisters to become his servants.

Milarepa's mother had a tiny piece of property of her own. She sold the land in order to buy an education in black magic for Milarepa so that he could avenge his family. Mastering the dark arts, Milarepa killed his uncle's eldest son and several others by willing the roof of a house to fall on them. He caused hailstorms to ruin his uncle's crops.

When the uncle finally returned Milarepa's property, Milarepa was so overcome by sorrow and guilt at what he had done that he gave up his property and went in search of a holy teacher. As penance, he was instructed by his teacher to build and then destroy a tower over and over again. Then his teacher advised him to become a monk and to live a life of contemplation. Milarepa lived for many years in a cave where he developed magical powers. Later in life, he wrote some of Tibet's most well-loved poetry and is now regarded as a Buddhist saint.

DEMON-PROWLER OF MOUNTAIN SHADOWS...DREADED MAN-BEAST OF TIBET...THE TERROR OF ALL THAT IS HUMAN!!

The Abominable Snowman of the Himalayas

WE DARE YOU TO SEE IT ALONE!

Each chilling moment a shock-test for your scare-endurance!!

FORREST TUCKER · PETER CUSHING

AUBREY BARING · VAL GUEST · NIGEL KNEALE · by NIGEL KNEALE · A REGALSCOPE PICTURE Released by 20th CENTURY-FOX

A movie poster for a 1957 British film reflects the twentieth-century Western fascination with the mysteries of Tibet.

the *Tibetan Book of the Dead*, which describes the journey of the soul through the forty-nine stages of bardo.

There are many long epic poems such as *Gesar,* the world's longest historical poem, or the songs of Milarepa, a much-revered Tibetan poet.

Folk literature is primarily preserved as an oral tradition. Storytelling was a family trade and wandering storytellers were in high demand in traditional Tibet. Folklore includes stories of Buddhist gods and goddesses, but also—like folklore everywhere—tales of animal tricksters, ghosts and demons, greedy and foolish humans, and creation myths.

Among the legends that Westerners associate the most with Tibet is the modern tale of Shangri-La, a fictitious paradise hidden in the Himalaya Mountains. This story was popularized by the 1933 novel *Lost Horizon* by the British author James Hilton. However, it has its roots in the centuries-old Tibetan Buddhist legend of Shambhala. Ancient texts describe this mythical kingdom, thought to be hidden inside the earth. Whether Shambhala was meant to be a physical, geographic place, or a visualization of a spiritual state isn't clear, but in the nineteenth- and early-twentieth centuries, Western adventurers and explorers journeyed to the mountains of Tibet in search of it.

Another myth or legend strongly associated with Tibet is that of the yeti. Sightings of the yeti, also called the abominable snowman, are rare, but tales of its existence abound. The apelike creature supposedly lives in caves in the high reaches of the Himalayas in Tibet, Nepal, and Bhutan. The word *yeti* derives from Tibetan words meaning "bear of the rocky place," or similar, and the peoples of the Himalayas have other names for the creature as well.

In 1985, members of a Chinese research society thought they had caught a yeti, but it turned out to be a rare macaque, 3.5 feet (1.06 m) tall, weighing 203 pounds (92.5 kg). Other supposed captures have proven to be hoaxes.

Some describe the yeti as a larger-than-human beast that walks upright. Indeed large footprints that appear to resemble humanlike feet have been found in the snowy landscape. Some scientists and explorers believe the real culprit is a Tibetan blue bear, the Himalayan brown bear, or the Asiatic black bear. (A related legendary creature is mythic American creature known as Bigfoot, which is said to roam the mountains of the American northwest.) The existence of the yeti has never been proved nor disproved, and like Shangri-La, it continues to fascinated and intrigue seekers around the world.

DANCE-DRAMA

Tibet has two dance traditions, one dedicated to religion and carried out during religious festivals, and the other a secular tradition performed by traveling groups of laymen. The religious dance-dramas were once amazing spectacles

that went on for days. They were performed in the courtyards of monasteries by the monks, who often trained for months to get the steps right. The arm movements were based on a form of yoga. Legend has it that one performer was able to make rocks explode and once set the Dalai Lama's robe on fire with the power of his dance steps. Dance-dramas were often accompanied by music, chanting, and spectacular costumes, including animal masks that represented good and evil spirits.

Cham dancers perform during Yuru Kabgyat, a Tibetan Buddhist festival held at a monastery in Ladakh, India.

The secular folk operas and plays performed by traveling groups also went on for days. Some were based on famous legends or events from the history of Tibet. Comics were part and parcel of the show and nobody escaped being lampooned, not even the lamas. Some of these plays and operas are being revived today.

MUSIC

Music has always been very important in the daily life of Tibetans. There are songs for almost every activity, from important occasions such as weddings to the routines of daily life such as plowing and even begging. Street songs, called *trom gyur shay* (TROM GIYUR shay), are popular contemporary songs that critique local politics or national events.

A unique set of instruments is employed to produce religious music. These musical instruments have religious significance as well. One such instrument is the thigh-bone trumpet, often made from a human thigh bone, which is used in a special ceremony called "cutting the go," where an individual attempts to give up all earthly needs and desires in order to reach enlightenment. Another instrument is the double-skull drum made of two human skulls with skins stretched over them. An attached bead strikes the two skins as the instrument is flipped from side to side. Conch shells and metal trumpets make a deep booming sound and are often used in religious ceremonies to accompany the chanting of scriptures.

INTERNET LINKS

www.bbc.com/earth/story/20150630-is-there-such-a-thing-as-a-yeti
This recent article gives the latest news on the legend of the yeti and its possible explanations.

www.bbc.co.uk/history/ancient/cultures/shangri_la_01.shtml
This page offers a good account of the Shangri-La tale.

www.buddhanet.net/tibart.htm
A good overview of Buddhist Art and Architecture.

www.metmuseum.org/toah/hd/tibu/hd_tibu.htm
The Metropolitan Museum of Art offers an overview of Tibetan Buddhist Art with an informative slide show.

www.norbulingka.org/thangka-painting.html
This site's information about thangka painting includes colorful examples.

www.pbs.org/mythsandheroes/myths_four_shangrila.html
This PBS special explores the legend of Shangri-La.

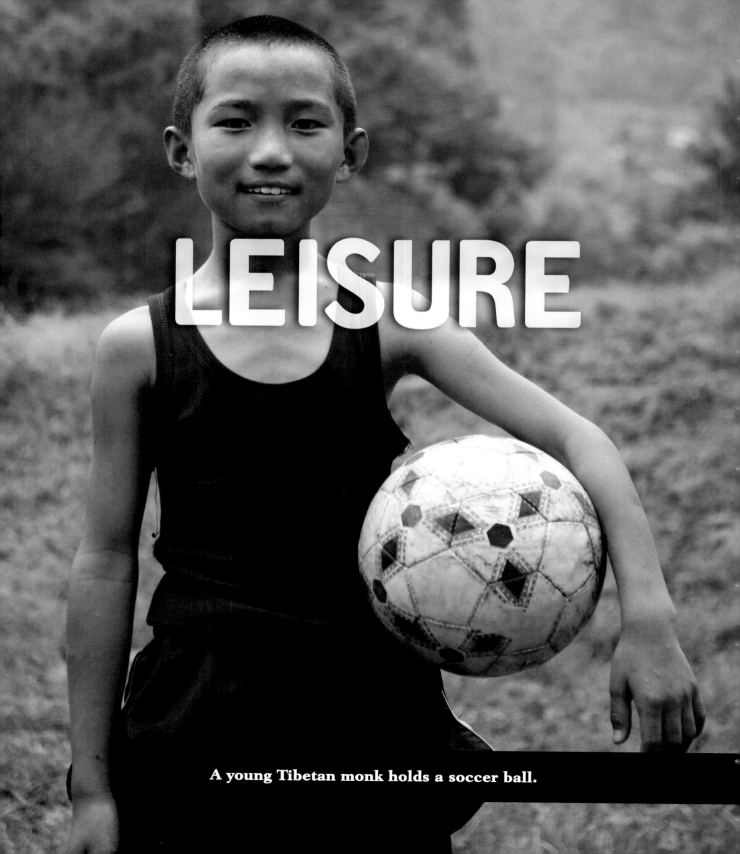

LEISURE

A young Tibetan monk holds a soccer ball.

11

S INCE THE CHINESE TAKEOVER OF Tibet, the concept of leisure time has changed. Before 1959, the distinction between religion and other aspects of daily life, such as leisure, was blurred. Common folk spent most of their day in prayer, working in the fields, or at home, and so there was little time for leisure. Today, the Chinese are importing many modern kinds of entertainment, from karaoke to soccer, both for themselves and for tourists.

Traditionally, Tibetans have enjoyed storytelling, gambling, and some sports, although not organized team games. Recently, modern leisure activities such as disco dancing and karaoke singing have been introduced. Reading was primarily a religious activity, as books were revered as sacred objects. This too has changed with the introduction of modern printing methods.

Nowadays some Tibetans dedicate their leisure time to rebuilding and refurbishing the many temple complexes damaged during the Cultural Revolution.

SPORTS

In the 1940s, sporting activities such as soccer and basketball were unheard of, but now basketball and soccer are being played all over Tibet

Tibetans enjoy picnicking so much that they have a festival for it, the Guolinka, or "Going Picnic" Festival. When the warm weather returns in late spring, people go outside for picnics and a host of outdoor activities. Typically the festival can last for several days.

In the village of Yunnan, villagers gather twice a month to chant Buddhist sutras and have a picnic.

and are almost as widespread as the popular Chinese pastime of table tennis. Tibet has a soccer team that plays in a Chinese league. Billiards has also arrived in Tibet and is played outdoors in front of tea shops or beer halls.

Travelers to Tibet in the 1950s described athletic contests between the dob dobs. These were small groups of athletic monks who specialized in three competitive sports—running, stone throwing, and broad jump. They wore loincloths and smeared their faces with soot to look more formidable. Groups like these, however, were very unusual, and Tibetan monks today generally spend very little time engaged in sports.

TIBETAN PICNICS

Picnics in Tibet are not just a matter of packing a picnic basket and setting off. The event is carefully organized several days ahead of time; it takes a long time to ferry all the necessities out to the picnic site by bicycle.

The richer families, or perhaps a work unit, erect their own huge appliquéd tents. These tents are beautiful works of art decorated with paintings of the wheel of life or other religious symbols. Furniture, rugs, and cushions are brought from the home and placed inside the tents. Food is cooked nearby and served throughout the day while the people lounge around and chat, eat, or play Tibetan board games. As the Tibetan beer begins to flow, storytelling begins as well. The stories can go on for hours and people come and go, hardly paying attention to the plot. Generally the story that is told is a traditional folk tale, like *The Ogress and the Monkey*, forgotten by all but the elderly.

As it gets dark, the dancing begins. Tibetan stamping dances mix with Chinese-style dancing or a version of disco. At night the whole party sleeps under the tent and the next day, when their heads have cleared from the excesses of the night before, the party continues.

YAK RACING

In addition to supplying food and livelihoods for many Tibetans, yaks also provide entertainment. Yak races are popular competitions at traditional festivals, particularly horse festivals. As in a horse race, a rider sits astride his yak and spurs it on to run the course. Yaks can run very quickly over short distances, making for quite a show as ten or twelve dash across an open field. The races can be dangerous, as yaks can respond unexpectedly to the cheers of the crowd, or the proximity of competing yaks. To add to the spectacle, the animals are decorated with red silks, flowers, and ornate saddles, and their riders are adorned in brightly colored costumes. Race winners take home a bit of money as well as respect and admiration.

GAMES

Girim (gee-RIM) is an ancient game, probably of Indian origin, that is played all over Tibet. It is similar to billiards and involves counters dusted in flour being flicked around a board. The object of the game is to get one's counters into one of the four pockets at the corners of the board.

Another popular game is *sho* (SHO), a game involving a circle of cowry shells. Counters are moved around the circle according to the throw of the dice. As the players rattle the dice in the cup, they recite a rhyme asking for the correct number to come up. Such games are played at picnics, during festivals, and whenever there is time for leisure.

Rickshaws are silhouetted against the bright lights of downtown Lhasa at night.

NIGHTLIFE IN LHASA

The Lhasa of old was a garden city full of trees and stone houses with intricately carved eaves and balconies. Beggars and domestic animals roamed the streets, and pilgrims walked around the holy places burning juniper wood as offerings. The Lhasa of today is a modern city with municipal water and sewage systems. Modern hotels with the attendant discos, karaoke bars, pool halls, movie theaters, and Chinese and Muslim restaurants dot the streets of the new city. The old town, however, remains untouched as if resistant to change.

SOCIALIZING

Socializing in some of the smaller towns happens when one or two families turn their living rooms into a temporary "bar and restaurant." Tibetans are a very friendly and hospitable people, and travelers and pilgrims can find shelter and hospitality wherever they go. Among nomadic groups, the evening's entertainment takes place wherever they stop for the night and consists of a campfire, lots of Tibetan tea and beer, food, and storytelling.

The center of social life in any town is the tea house, where groups of friends spend evenings or afternoons together. Money is pooled in the center of the table and the tea servers go around refilling the cups with Chinese tea as often as necessary, taking the cost from the pile.

Tea drinking is an important social event in Tibet. Tibetan tea is a meal in itself, full of barley flour and butter and whatever else that is considered necessary for the occasion. Visitors are always offered tea when they visit a home and it is impolite not to accept it. Custom dictates that the cup should be refilled as long as the visit lasts.

INTERNET LINKS

www.businessinsider.com/20-striking-photos-of-daily-life-in-tibet-2016-2
This slide show includes interesting photos of daily life in Tibet.

www.npr.org/sections/pictureshow/2010/09/17/129930953/monks
"A Day in the Life of a Tibetan Monk" is a photo story.

kaleidoscope.cultural-china.com/en/142Kaleidoscope3460.html
This is a quick look at yak racing with some photos.

www.tibettravel.org/tibetan-local-customs/yak-racing-in-tibet.html
This site offers a short article on yak racing

www.tibettravel.org/tibetan-people/tea-life-in-tibet.html
This article discusses the importance of tea in everyday life in Tibet, with links to other related topics.

FESTIVALS

Chinese dancers perform for Serf Emancipation Day festivities in Lhasa.

12

ONE OF THE NEWEST PUBLIC holidays in the Tibet Autonomous Region is Serf Emancipation Day on March 28. This annual special day was introduced in 2009 to celebrate the fiftieth year of Communist Chinese liberation of—or control of—Tibet. According to the Chinese, the day celebrates the end of the Tibetan feudal society and serfdom. The Dalai Lama has denounced the holiday, not in defense of serfdom, but because he says it distracts from the day's true purpose, which is to honor Chinese nationalism and the takeover of Tibet.

There are many festivals in the Tibetan calendar, and most of them are religious in nature. These festivals would once have been national celebrations, with people from all over Tibet congregating in the towns to participate in the festivities. Nomads would bring in products for trade and the streets would fill up with pilgrims. For twenty years or so after the Chinese took over, all such activities were put to a stop, but with the recent new freedom to practice religion, some of these ancient festivals have reappeared again. However, among the laypeople, only a few old men can fully grasp the significance of the rites in these events.

Many public holidays in Tibet are Chinese holidays, such as Chinese New Year and Tomb Sweeping Day, which might mean little to Tibetans, but the government offices and banks are closed on these days.

THE TIBETAN CALENDAR

The Tibetan calendar is based on the phases of the moon rather than the earth's revolution around the sun. Because of this, the Tibetan year begins sometime in February, just as the traditional Chinese year does. Since lunar cycles take less than thirty days, additional days are included in the calendar at auspicious times to coordinate the seasons and the months. Tibet's calendar has twelve or thirteen months, but some of these may not actually take place if the stars suggest that the month may be a bad one. One tourist staying in Tibet reported that during his stay the month equivalent to July was abandoned and instead there were two Augusts.

The Tibetan calendar begins with the birth of the Buddha and runs in sixty-year cycles. Each year is represented by one of the five mystical elements—fire, earth, iron, water, or wood—and one of twelve animals—hare, dragon, snake, horse, sheep, monkey, bird, dog, pig, rat, ox, and tiger. Each element is associated with two consecutive years, the first is a "male" year and the next is "female." For example, 1940 was the year of the Male Iron Dragon and 1941 was the year of the Female Iron Snake.

TIBETAN NEW YEAR'S EVE

The Tibetan New Year, or Losar, celebrations begin on the first day of the first lunar month, which usually corresponds to the end of January or early February. But before the day arrives, people begin to prepare for the New Year by cleaning their houses and buying new material to make quilt covers and clothes. In the kitchen, the women busy themselves making special New Year pastries called *khabtse* (CAB-tse), which are left as offerings at the temple and given to visitors.

The house is decorated with eight auspicious signs, including conch shells (signifying the Buddha's enlightenment), dharma wheels (a wheel with eight or more spokes), and eternal knots (signifying love and harmony). A swastika, the symbol of luck, is painted on the front door, and the ceiling beams are painted with white dots to encourage long life and good harvests. On the eve of Losar, the house is swept clean and the dust piled into a corner. On top of

the pile of dust are placed tiny effigies of evil spirits made out of dough. When the women have braided their hair and everyone has dressed in new clothes, the family sits down to the last meal of the year. A soup called *guthuk* (GUH-thuk) is prepared especially for the occasion.

After the meal, the oldest member of the family rubs a ball of dough over each family member to draw out all the illnesses they had been afflicted with in the past year. Following this, the whole family carries the pile of dust out of the house, where it is thrown into a communal fire. The sweeping away of the dust symbolizes the family getting rid of the demons that dwell in their home. When the dust is thrown on the fire, family members will shout and set off fireworks to ensure that the demons do not return.

When the Dalai Lamas ruled Tibet, there were ritual dances, horse races, and archery competitions to usher in the New Year. Some of these traditions are beginning to return, most notably an annual horseback riding tournament. In the competition, horsemen ride toward a target and try to hit it with a bow and arrow and then with a musket.

Fireworks welcome the Tibetan New Year on February 19, 2015, in Lhasa.

Monks perform on musical instruments made of conch shells on the first day of the Tibetan new year.

NEW YEAR'S DAY

All Tibetans get up very early on New Year's Day and dress in their best clothes. (For many years, everyone had to wear green or gray work clothes, but recently more people can be seen wearing their ethnic costumes.) People visit each other's houses, and at each house they are offered wheat and tsampa from an offering box. New prayer flags are printed on brightly colored cloth and are hung from the rooftops. Family members link hands and walk around the flat roof of their house, throwing handfuls of beer and barley dough as an offering and calling "*La le go*" (la-LE-go), or "Victory to the gods."

Once the house visits are done, families make their way to the Potala Palace. Pilgrims climb the hundreds of steps to the top of the palace, turning prayer wheels as they go and chanting mantras to help them focus on their devotion to Buddha. When passing by particular statues or sacred objects, the pilgrims prostrate themselves in reverence.

MONLAM

Monlam is a prayer festival (usually in February) that lasts fifteen days. In Lhasa, the Potala is the center of the festival's activities, which include prayer ceremonies, religious examinations, and dances. During this period, student-monks working toward the rank of *geshe* (GE-shay) debate with their seniors, pilgrims bring huge sacks of offerings to the temple, and weary travelers sleep in the streets of Lhasa, lighting fires to keep warm. The fifteenth day, the Butter Lamp Festival, originated when the fifth Dalai Lama

had a dream of paradise and modeled it in butter to show his followers what it looked like.

In the past every noble family made a sculpture out of butter and donated it to the temple. Today the responsibility for making these sculptures has been passed on to the monks. Huge dragons and lotus flowers and mythological figures surround images of the Buddha, all of them carved out of Tibetan butter, which has a consistency similar to that of cheese. Pilgrims circle the sculptures, repeating their prayers all night long. As the sun rises, the butter sculptures begin to melt, yet again symbolizing the Buddhist belief in the transient nature of everything.

The Monlam Festival ends with a parade of the statue of Jampa, the future Buddha, around the main square in Lhasa. The parade is accompanied by the sound of a Tibetan orchestra. Pilgrims cover the statue in silk scarves as a sign of respect before the statue is returned to the temple.

Monks take part in a special "Great Prayer" during the Monlam Festival.

THE GOLDEN STAR FESTIVAL

A Festival of the Lamps celebration attracts both monks and tourists.

For the monks, the months leading up to the Golden Star Festival are spent inside the monasteries to avoid killing any newly born insects whose incarnation might be prematurely ended if they are stepped on. The Golden Star Festival, or Bathing Festival, celebrates the cleansing away of passion, greed, and jealousy. The monks come out of the temples to be treated to drama and opera performances organized by townsfolk. In the past, these operas and plays would have been performed by groups of amateur actors from all over Tibet, who put on these shows as payment for part of their village's taxes. These days, performances by state-run dance and drama groups are staged. The monks are given yogurt as part of the banquet prepared for them. Families and work units arrange three- or four-day-long picnics in the parks surrounding the Potala Palace, sleeping under beautiful canopies, eating, and playing games. The festival is also marked by ritual bathing and the ritual washing of clothes in the river.

OTHER FESTIVALS

The four great seasonal Buddhist festivals are Losar, Saga Dawa, Chokor Duchen, and Lhabab Duchen. During these times, the effects of positive or negative actions are said to be multiplied ten million times. Chokor Duchen, for example, falls on the fourth day of the sixth lunar month, and it commemorates the Buddha's first sermon. On this day, monasteries display huge thangkas on the monastery walls, and the day is spent in prayer. Some pilgrims spend the day climbing Tibet's holy mountains.

The Festival of the Lamps commemorates the death of Tsongkapa, the founder of the Yellow Hat school of Buddhism. Fires are lit on the roofs of the monasteries, and people light lamps and butter candles in his memory.

The Scapegoat Festival, which takes place on the twenty-eighth day of the second lunar month, is a spectacular event accompanied by a ritualistic dance-drama. The festival begins with a procession of monks in black robes. This is followed by troupes of dancers dressed in costumes and wearing huge masks depicting demonic faces, whirling and shrieking to the accompaniment of discordant music. Dancers dressed as saints chase away these demons and perform a more stately and dignified dance. A figure made of dough and filled with colored dough entrails is then torn to pieces. This is the scapegoat; it represents all the evils of the world.

INTERNET LINKS

www.chinahighlights.com/tibet/tibetan-festival-date.htm
A calendar of events for the current year is listed on this page, with links to fuller articles.

www.chinatibettrain.com/tibetfestivals.htm
Tibetan festivals, with vibrant photos, are featured on this Chinese tourism site.

blog.classictravel.net.cn/blog/category/tibet
This Chinese travel site has colorful photos of several Tibetan festivals.

www.reuters.com/article/us-china-tibet-serfs-idUSTRE52Q05U20090327
Serf Emancipation Day and the question of Tibetan serfdom is covered in this article.

FOOD

Nuts, raisins, and dried tomatoes are set out for sale in a food stall.

13

N MANY REGIONS OF TIBET, THE harsh, rocky environment is not suited to growing a wide range of vegetables and fruits. The Tibetan diet, by necessity, has developed by making the most of what is available. However, religious restrictions further limit the possibilities for many people. Tibetan Buddhism prohibits the eating of fish, for example, and Tibetan Islam limits certain meats.

During the 1960s and 1970s, Tibet experienced severe food shortages as the Chinese authorities tried to impose a system of communal farming all across China. Farmers had to plant wheat instead of the hardier barley, which is better suited to Tibet's climate. The thin, under-fertilized soil was unable to support the intensive farming methods introduced by the Chinese. The situation at that time was very grave and a famine ensued.

Today, in addition to the communes, people are allowed to own their own farms and yaks again and the nomads are back on the northern plain roaming with their herds. Barley has replaced wheat once more, and a greater variety of food has come to Tibet from the rest of China.

YAK PRODUCTS

The great staple of the Tibetan diet is yak meat. The sturdy yak, a little like a cross between a cow and a buffalo, has provided the basic necessities of life for Tibetan people for thousands of years. On the Northern Plateau, yak meat a mainstay of people's diet because vegetables do not grow in the dry, cold climate. In the southern part of the country, yak meat is often supplemented by vegetables, nuts and fruits, and the second staple—barley.

Yaks provide much more than just food for the Tibetans. The hide is used to make clothes, bags, shoes, and tents. Even the bones are turned into utensils and jewelry. Besides meat, Tibetans also depend on their yaks for dairy products. The female yak produces milk with a very high fat content. Unlike people in other countries, Tibetans do not worry about high cholesterol levels; fat is an essential part of the diet in Tibet. The extreme cold and strenuous manual work that characterize their daily lives mean that Tibetans need a high calorie diet, making yak milk an invaluable food item.

A couple sells yak butter at the market on Barkhor Street in Lhasa.

BUTTER Yak milk is used primarily to make butter. The milk is emptied into a butter churn, an essential part of Tibetan kitchen equipment, where it is stirred, or churned, until it begins to thicken. Once the milk solidifies, it is wrapped in skins and taken to the market to be sold. Sealed in the skins, it keeps for long periods. When the skins are opened, the butter begins to decay, producing veins of mold similar to blue cheese. But this process is much slower than it is in most cheese-producing countries because the cold, dry weather does not encourage the growth of mold.

CHEESE After butter, the most important use for yak milk is to make cheese. The milk is first boiled and poured into a mold. A setting agent is added to ensure that the milk solidifies. Once the cheese grows a hard outer rind, it is stored for many months. When the cheese is ready for consumption, it is cut into cubes, which are strung together like beads in a necklace. Although yak cheese is very hard, it is also very nutritious and sweeter than the types of cheese we are more familiar with. Yak cheese is so hard that it can take up to an hour of chewing before it is soft enough to swallow.

Yak meat hangs in a butcher's market on the street in Lhasa.

YOGURT Yak milk is also used to make yogurt. Today this is a rare delicacy in southern Tibet but it can still be bought in the markets for a high price. The test for good yogurt is to turn it upside down. If the yogurt does not fall out of the jar, it is fresh and good. During the summer, yogurt plays an important part in the Golden Star Festival, when it is served to monks who have been cloistered in their monasteries for weeks.

To make yogurt, yak milk from the evening milking is boiled and left to settle with a tiny bit of yogurt. Overnight, the live bacteria act on the fresh milk, turning the milk into fresh yogurt. Some of this is added to the next batch, made in the morning. When it is available, sugar is added to sweeten the yogurt.

YAK MEAT Similar to beef except slightly stronger in taste, yak meat is becoming a tourist favorite. In countries like Nepal, it is now possible to order a yak steak or a yak burger. But yak meat is typically served in its dried form in Tibet. In a country where freezers and electricity are a luxury, the best means of preserving the goodness of the meat is to hang it up in the dry, almost germ-free Tibetan air. When the meat is needed, it is sliced off the carcass and eaten as is or added to a thick stew.

FOOD TABOOS

Goats, sheep, and chickens are bred, but they are less popular than yaks because they are smaller animals and therefore necessitate more slaughter per pound of meat. The slaughtering of animals is handled by Tibet's Muslims, who butcher the animals according to Islamic customs. Occupations such as these are abhorred by Tibetan Buddhists, whose religion forbids them from killing unnecessarily. If the slaughter of an animal is necessary for the survival of the family, the Tibetan Buddhist will say a quick prayer over the animal before killing it.

Tsampa balls are served with fruit yogurt.

Because of Tibetan funeral customs, fishing is forbidden. Although less common than other burial methods, the bodies of the dead are sometimes thrown into rivers to be consumed by fishes as a gesture that signifies the act of giving back what one has taken from this world. The eating of fish is therefore objectionable to Tibetan Buddhists. For the Chinese, however, fish is a delicacy and a common ingredient in Chinese cooking.

GRAINS AND VEGETABLES

Barley flour is a staple for most Tibetans. Barley is a hardy plant that can survive in poor soil and dry conditions, so it is widely grown in Tibet. After they are harvested, barley grains are roasted in small quantities in hot sand over a stove and then ground. The flour has a nutty taste, and when mixed with Tibetan tea becomes a meal in itself, called *tsampa*. The bowl is turned with one hand while the other hand kneads the flour in the hot tea mixture until it becomes a soft dough ball. The ball is then eaten like a soft donut. Yogurt, sugar, or raisins can be added to give a sweet flavor. Because the grains have been roasted, it does not taste raw.

Wheat, although grown in Tibet, is less hardy than barley and is more of a luxury item. It is used to make unleavened bread, noodles, and a fine, thin pastry covering for small pies and cakes. Rarer still are grains, such as buckwheat and corn, which are a part of the diet in some regions. They are ground into flour and made into bread.

In many parts of Tibet green vegetables are a rarity and are only available as canned imports. In the south, green vegetables such as cabbage are grown and some wild plants are gathered for food, especially nettles, which are often a large part of the diet of hermit monks. Herbs too are gathered from the wild, both for medicine and to flavor food. Chilies are an important flavoring in Tibetan cuisine and are also eaten as snacks—like fresh chilies smeared with lard.

Fruits such as pears, apples, peaches, and tangerines are grown in Tibet. In the cities, these are available dried, as are figs, raisins, persimmons, cashew nuts, and peanuts.

Tibetan farm workers inspect the crops in a barley field.

SOME TIBETAN DISHES

Everyone carries with them their store of ground barley flour, a string of cheese cubes, perhaps some sugar, the ingredients for tea, and a wooden

Momos are a favorite traditional Tibetan dumpling.

bowl. All that is then needed to make a typical Tibetan meal is some hot water, butter, and salt.

A more substantial evening meal might consist of wheat flour noodles cooked in boiling water with the addition of onion, chilies, and pieces of meat. Eggs are often eaten hard-boiled or made into an omelet with vegetables and chili peppers.

A special dish eaten on the eve of the New Year is a thick stew made from meat and vegetables and thickened with barley flour. This dish is called *guthuk*. Another festive delicacy is called *momos* (MOH-mohs). These are steamed dumplings made from thin sheets of wheat flour wrapped around spiced meat.

The few restaurants that cater to tourists usually serve Chinese Sichuan dishes. These include stir-fried pieces of meat and vegetables cooked very quickly with chili.

TIBETAN TEA

Tibetan tea is by all accounts an acquired taste. It is made from tea leaves, butter, salt, and barley flour. First, the tea is boiled in a huge pot with wood ash soda (added to bring out the color) until the dried leaves have infused the water. The tea is strained into a large wooden pot that resembles a butter churn, and melted butter and salt are added. A plunger is inserted and pumped to emulsify the butter, and finally barley flour is added before the whole mixture is churned.

The result is a thin, savory beverage. When the tea is first poured into drinking bowls, a layer of butter floats to the top. This is skimmed off and is either kept for animal fodder or recycled for the next brew by the very poor. The tea maker makes gallons of tea at a time, and it is always kept on hand. Visitors are always offered tea, and it is considered impolite to refuse the offer.

OTHER DRINKS

In bigger towns, teahouses sell Chinese tea sweetened with imported sugar and milk. The main alcoholic drink is *chang*—homemade beer brewed from fermented barley. It has a sour taste and low alcohol content. The same mixture is often distilled into a spirit called *arak* (a-RACK), which is much more potent. There are also many imported alcoholic drinks in the bars of Lhasa, especially the Chinese beer called Tsingtao, as well as Chinese versions of cola and carbonated fruit drinks.

INTERNET LINKS

www.nytimes.com/2012/02/22/dining/momos-tibetans-forbidden-special-treat.html?_r=0
This *New York Times* article includes recipes.

www.seriouseats.com/2015/09/tibetan-cuisine-introduction-dishes-to-know.html
This excellent introduction to Tibetan cuisine includes many photographs.

simplytibetan.com
This Tibetan cooking blog has recipes and step-by-step photos.

DRESIL (TIBETAN SWEET RICE)

Dresil is a traditional Tibetan dessert eaten during Losar, the Tibetan New Year. In Tibet, it is made with *dri*, which is butter made from female yak milk. You can substitute butter made from cow's or goat's milk in place of the dri. This popular dish is often cooked with *droma*, a root vegetable that tastes a bit like sweet potato.

2 cups (340 g) of white rice (basmati works well)
6 tablespoons (89 g) of butter
½ cup (170 g) of cashews
1 cup (128 g) of raisins
¼ cup (32 g) of sugar
Chopped dates or any other nuts or dried fruits, as desired

Cook the white rice. While it is warm, melt in the butter and stir in the cashews, raisins, and sugar. Serve the dresil in small bowls alongside sweet tea or *po cha*.

PO CHA (TIBETAN BUTTER TEA)

The salt and butter in *po cha* give this beverage its unique flavor.

4 cups (946 milliliters) of water
2 teabags of plain black tea
¼ teaspoon (1 gram) of salt
2 tablespoons (30 g) of butter
⅓ cup (79 mL) of half-and-half or milk

In a saucepan, bring the water to a boil. Add the two teabags and let them steep for a few minutes while the water continues to boil. Remove the teabags. Add the salt and half-and-half. Remove the liquid from the heat.

Carefully pour the tea mixture, along with the butter, into a blender. Blend for about one minute. Serve the tea right away, since po cha is best when served hot!

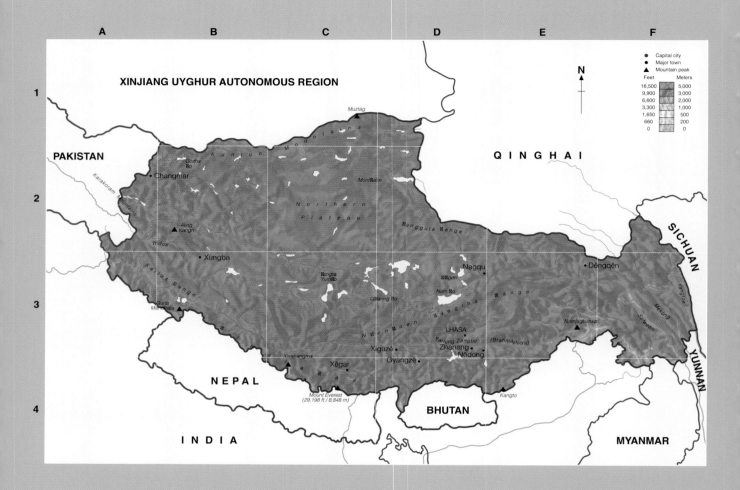

XINJIANG UYGHUR AUTONOMOUS REGION

PAKISTAN

QINGHAI

N

Capital city
Major town
Mountain peak

Feet   Meters
16,500   5,000
9,900   3,000
6,600   2,000
3,300   1,000
1,650   500
660   200
0   0

Muztag

Kunlun Mountains

Gozha Co

•Changmar

Mont Naim

Karakoram Mountains

Indus

Northern
Plateau

Tanggula Range

SICHUAN

Aling
Kangri

•Xungba

Tangra
Yumco

Nagqu

•Dêngqên

Yangtze

Kailas Range

Qilaring Co

Nyainrong

Mekong

Namjagbarwa

Gurla
Mandhata

Nam Co

Nyenchen Tangha Range

Salween

YUNNAN

Xixabangma

LHASA

Yarlung Zangbo

•Xigazê

Zhanang

(Brahmaputra)

Nêdong

•Gyangzê

NEPAL

Xêgar

Mount Everest
(29,198 ft / 8,848 m)

BHUTAN

Kangto

INDIA

MYANMAR

MAP OF TIBET

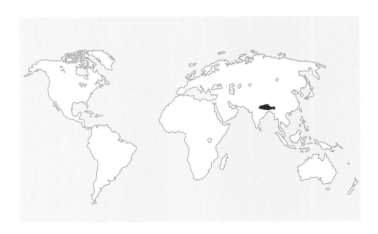

ECONOMIC TIBET

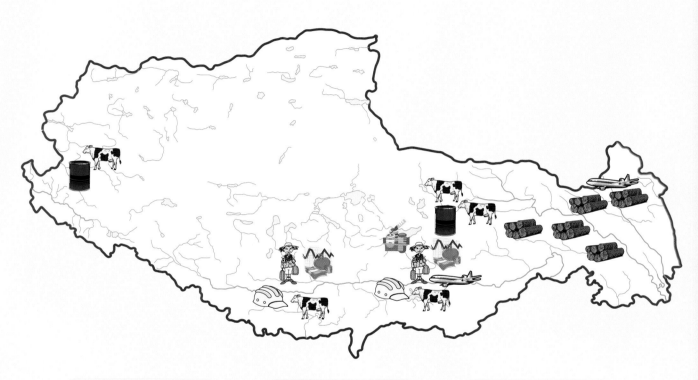

Services

 Airport

 Financial Services

 Research Centers

 Tourism

Agriculture

 Farms

Natural Resources

 Mines

 Oil and Gas

 Timber

ABOUT THE ECONOMY

OVERVIEW

Many Tibetans still make their living as farmers, nomadic herdsmen, or traders. They have benefited from the steady improvements in irrigation as well as the land management policies of the central government. As a result of the Chinese government's efforts to boost the local economy, the number of Tibetans finding employment in sectors ranging from the service industry and education to even technological research is increasing. There is also a large pool of ethnic Chinese workers in and around Lhasa. They are mainly employed in the civil service, the military, and the private sector.

GROSS DOMESTIC PRODUCT (GDP)

$15 billion (2014)

GDP PER CAPITA

$4,766 (2014)

GDP GROWTH

11 percent (2016 estimate)

CURRENCY

Chinese yuan renminbi (CNY)
1 yuan = 10 jiao
1 jiao = 10 fen
Notes: 1, 2, 5, 10, 20, 50 and 100 yuan

Coins: 1, 2 and 5 jiao; and 1, 2, and 5 fen
I USD = 6.59 yuan (June 2016)

LAND USE

Tibet has extensive forest areas, with primary industrial centers and more intensive agricultural settlements largely located around Lhasa, Nyingchi, Shannan, and Xigaze. Petroleum and natural gas mines are found around Naqu and Ali, in northern Tibet.

MINERAL RESOURCES

Salt, gold, iron, copper, borax, uranium, chromites

AGRICULTURAL PRODUCTS

Barley, wheat, buckwheat, rye, potatoes, fruits, vegetables

MAJOR EXPORTS

Timber, handicrafts, clothing, quilts, fabrics, carpets, toys, wooden goods

MAJOR IMPORTS

Building materials, machinery, electronic goods, chemical products, food products

MAIN TRADE PARTNERS

China, Hong Kong, Nepal, India, Great Britain, South Africa, Brazil, United States

WORKFORCE

1.37 million (2000 estimate)

UNEMPLOYMENT RATE

4.1 percent in urban areas (2013 estimate)

CULTURAL TIBET

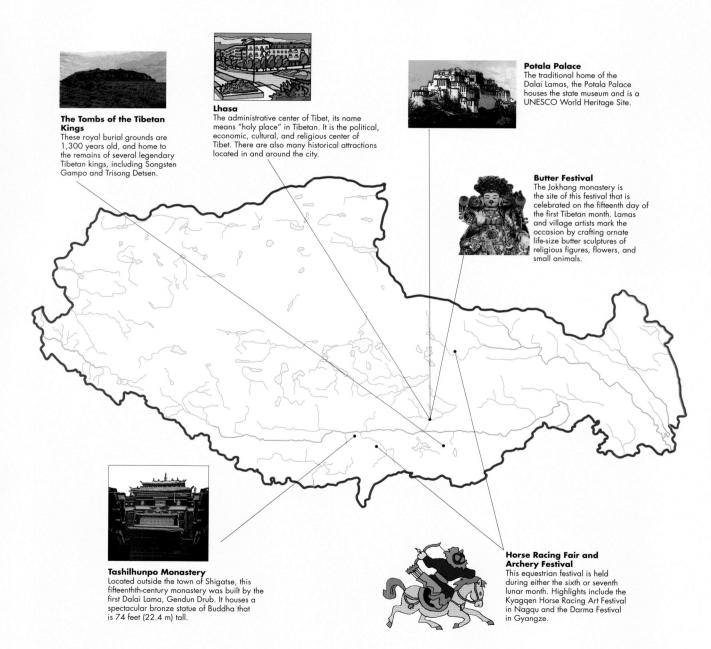

The Tombs of the Tibetan Kings
These royal burial grounds are 1,300 years old, and home to the remains of several legendary Tibetan kings, including Songsten Gampo and Trisong Detsen.

Lhasa
The administrative center of Tibet, its name means "holy place" in Tibetan. It is the political, economic, cultural, and religious center of Tibet. There are also many historical attractions located in and around the city.

Potala Palace
The traditional home of the Dalai Lamas, the Potala Palace houses the state museum and is a UNESCO World Heritage Site.

Butter Festival
The Jokhang monastery is the site of this festival that is celebrated on the fifteenth day of the first Tibetan month. Lamas and village artists mark the occasion by crafting ornate life-size butter sculptures of religious figures, flowers, and small animals.

Tashilhunpo Monastery
Located outside the town of Shigatse, this fifteenthth-century monastery was built by the first Dalai Lama, Gendun Drub. It houses a spectacular bronze statue of Buddha that is 74 feet (22.4 m) tall.

Horse Racing Fair and Archery Festival
This equestrian festival is held during either the sixth or seventh lunar month. Highlights include the Kyagqen Horse Racing Art Festival in Nagqu and the Darma Festival in Gyangze.

ABOUT THE CULTURE

OFFICIAL NAME
Tibet Autonomous Region

FLAG DESCRIPTION
A large yellow star and four smaller yellow stars in the upper hoist-side corner set on a red background.

TOTAL AREA
474,300 square miles (1.23 million sq km)

ADMINSTRATIVE CENTER
Lhasa

POPULATION
3,180,000 (2014)

ETHNIC GROUPS
Ethnic Tibetans, 90 percent; Han Chinese, 8 percent; Monpa, 0.3 percent; Hui, 0.3 percent; others, 0.2 percent. (2014)

MAIN RELIGIOUS GROUPS
Buddhism, Bön

LIFE EXPECTANCY
68.2 years (2013)

BIRTH RATE
15.8 births per 1,000 Tibetans (2013)

DEATH RATE
6.8 deaths per 1,000 Tibetans (2013)

MAIN LANGUAGES
Tibetan, Mandarin

LITERACY RATE
62 percent (2010 estimate)

NATIONAL HOLIDAYS
National Day (March 10), International Labor Day (May 1), Death of Gautama Buddha (February 8)

LEADERS IN POLITICS
Tenzin Gyatsom, b. 1935, 14th Dalai Lama, 1950—present, in exile
Gedhun Choekyi Nyima, b. 1989, Panchen Lama since 1995, abducted by Chinese officials and missing since 1995
Gyaincain Norbu, b. 1990, Panchen Lama since 1995, installed by the Chinese government; his legitimacy is challenged
Losang Jamcan, Chairman of Tibet Autonomous Region, 2013—present
Chen Quanguo, top official and Communist Party Chief of Tibet Autonomous Region, 2011—present

TIMELINE

IN TIBET	IN THE WORLD
	116–117 CE The Roman Empire reaches its greatest extent.
127 BCE Start of Yarlung dynasty	
Early seventh century CE Tibetan Empire rises in power.	**600 CE** Height of Mayan civilization
627 King Songtsen Gampo reigns.	
641 Buddhism is introduced to Tibetans.	
670 Tibet wages war with Tang China.	
836 Bön priests oppose Buddhism.	
842 King Langdarma is assassinated.	
	1000 The Chinese perfect gunpowder and begin to use it in warfare.
1270 Kublai Khan, emperor of China, converts to Tibetan Buddhism.	
1391 The first Dalai Lama, Gedun Drub, is born.	
	1558–1603 Reign of Elizabeth I of England
	1620 Pilgrims sail the *Mayflower* to America.
	1776 US Declaration of Independence
	1789–1799 The French Revolution
	1861 The US Civil War begins.
	1869 The Suez Canal opens.
1910 About two thousand Chinese troops invade Lhasa. The thirteenth Dalai Lama escapes to India.	
1912–1913 An uprising against the Chinese erupts; Tibet declares independence.	**1914–1919** World War I

IN TIBET	IN THE WORLD
	1939–1945 World War II
	1949
1950–1951 Chinese troops from the People's Republic of China invade Tibet; Tibet becomes part of China.	The North Atlantic Treaty Organization (NATO) is formed.
	1957 The Russians launch *Sputnik*.
1959 The fourteenth Dalai Lama escapes to India with eighty thousand Tibetans and sets up a government-in-exile in India. China appoints a military government in Tibet and raids monasteries.	**1966–1969** The Chinese Cultural Revolution
	1986
1989 The Dalai Lama is awarded the Nobel Peace Prize.	Nuclear power disaster at Chernobyl in Ukraine
	1991 Breakup of the Soviet Union
1996 Human rights campaign protests the mistreatment of Tibetan dissidents.	**1997** Hong Kong is returned to China.
2002 Representatives of the Dalai Lama are invited to Beijing for talks.	**2001** Terrorists crash planes in New York, Washington, DC, and Pennsylvania.
	2003 War in Iraq begins.
2006 The Qinghai-Tibet Railway, linking Tibet with the rest of China, is completed.	**2008** The United States elects its first African American president, Barack Obama.
2011 Tibetan Buddhist monks begin series of self-immolations in protest against Chinese abuses. Dalai Lama retires from politics; Lobsang Sangay elected to lead government-in-exile.	
2013 Number of protest self-immolations rises to over one hundred.	**2015–2016** Islamist terrorist attacks in France and Belgium
2016 US president Barack Obama meets with Dalai Lama despite Chinese objections.	

GLOSSARY

Bhotia
A group of people who are ethnically Tibetan but live within the borders of India.

Bön
The earliest known form of religion in Tibet.

chang
A nourishing Tibetan drink made from barley, similar to beer.

chuba (CHOO-pa)
An overcoat, often made of sheepskin, traditionally worn in Himalayan countries.

dob dobs (DOB dobs)
Small groups of monks who took part in competitions to test their athletic prowess.

dzo (ZO)
A cross between a yak and a cow.

Gelukpa
The Yellow Hat Buddhist sect, which ruled Tibet politically and spiritually before the invasion of the Chinese. Its spiritual head is the Dalai Lama.

geshe (GE-shay)
A monk who has passed the initial stages of progress toward lamahood.

girim (gee-RIM)
An ancient Indian game played all over Tibet.

guthuk (GUH-thuk)
A thick soup-stew eaten at New Year's.

Lamaism
The name given to Tibetan Buddhism, which depends heavily on spiritual guidance from a spiritual leader called a lama.

mandala
A complex geometric pattern representing some aspect of Buddhist religion.

mantra
A sacred formula repeated as an incantation in meditation.

Pinyin
The system for representing the sound of a Chinese word in Roman characters.

Shangri-La
A mythical, mystical Himalayan paradise described in the 1933 novel *Lost Horizon* by James Hilton.

sho (SHO)
A popular Tibetan game in which rhymes are recited when the dice are thrown.

thangkas (THANG-kas)
Banners hung on monastery walls during religious festivals.

tsampa (tsam-PA)
Tibetan bread that is made from barley flour, tea, and butter.

tsha tsha (CHA cha)
A small medallion made of clay worn as an amulet.

FOR FURTHER INFORMATION

BOOKS

Dalai Lama, and Galen Rowell. *My Tibet*. Berkeley, CA: University of California Press, 1995.

Gyatso, Tenzin. *Freedom in Exile: The Autobiography of the Dalai Lama*. New York: HarperPerennial, 2008.

Harrer, Heinrich. *Seven Years in Tibet*. New York: TarcherPerigee, 2009.

Mayhew, Bradley, and Robert Kelly. *Lonely Planet Tibet*, 9th edition. New York: Lonely Planet, 2015.

Pistono, Matteo. *In the Shadow of the Buddha: One Man's Journey of Discovery in Tibet*. New York: Dutton, 2011.

Schaik, Sam van. *Tibet: A History*. New Haven, CT: Yale University Press, 2011.

DVDS/FILMS

Kundun. DVD. Walt Disney Video, 1997.

Mountain Patrol: Kekexili. Sony Pictures Home Entertainment, 2006.

Seven Years in Tibet. DVD. Sony Pictures, 1997.

Tibetan Warrior. DVD. Garden Thieves Pictures. 2015.

MUSIC

Tibet, Tibet. Yungchen Lhamo. Real World Records, 2012.

Tibetan Sacred Temple Music. Tibetan Monks of Drepung Loseling Monastery, Allegro Corporation, 1990.

WEBSITES

BBC News. Tibet profile. www.bbc.com/news/world-asia-pacific-16689779

Central Tibetan Administration, official site of the Tibetan government-in-exile. tibet.net

Free Tibet. www.freetibet.org

Lonely Planet: Tibet. www.lonelyplanet.com/china/tibet

New York Times, The. www.nytimes.com/topic/destination/tibet

Travel China Guide. www.travelchinaguide.com/cityguides/tibet

BIBLIOGRAPHY

BBC News Tibet profile. http://www.bbc.com/news/world-asia-pacific-16689779.

Central Tibetan Administration, official site of the Tibetan government in exile. http://tibet.net.

China Tibet Online. http://eng.tibet.cn/index.shtml.

Hessler, Peter. "Tibet Through Chinese Eyes." *The Atlantic*, February 1999. http://www.theatlantic.com/magazine/archive/1999/02/tibet-through-chinese-eyes/306395.

Human Rights Watch. "China: Attempts to Seal Off Tibet from Outside Information." July 13, 2012. https://www.hrw.org/news/2012/07/13/china-attempts-seal-tibet-outside-information.

Jones, Lucy. "Is the Himalayan Yeti a Real Animal?" BBC Earth. June 30, 2015. http://www.bbc.com/earth/story/20150630-is-there-such-a-thing-as-a-yeti.

Lonely Planet: Tibet. https://www.lonelyplanet.com/china/tibet.

Mishra, Pankaj. "Celebrating Tibet's Culture." *Travel & Leisure*. http://www.travelandleisure.com/articles/higher-ground.

Roberts, Dexter. "Tibet Can't Kick Its Subsidy Habit." *Bloomberg Businessweek*, December 16, 2015. http://www.bloomberg.com/news/articles/2015-12-17/tibet-s-potemkin-economy.

Shakya, Tsering. "The Myth of Shangri-la." Tibetan Buddhism in the West, originally published in 1991. http://info-buddhism.com/Myth_of_Shangri-la_Tsering_Shakya.html.

Sperling, Elliot. "Don't Know Much About Tibetan History." *The New York Times*, April 13, 2008. http://www.nytimes.com/2008/04/13/opinion/13sperling.html?_r=0.

UNESCO, World Heritage Centre. "Historic Ensemble of the Potala Palace, Lhasa." http://whc.unesco.org/en/list/707.

Wan, William, and Xu Yangjingjing. "China promotes mixed marriages in Tibet as way to achieve 'unity'." *The Washington Post*, August 16, 2014. https://www.washingtonpost.com/world/asia_pacific/china-promotes-mixed-marriages-in-tibet-as-way-to-achieve-unity/2014/08/16/94409ca6-238e-11e4-86ca-6f03cbd15c1a_story.html.

Wong, Edward. "Tibetans Fight to Salvage Fading Culture in China." *The New York Times*, Nov. 28, 2015. http://www.nytimes.com/2015/11/29/world/asia/china-tibet-language-education.html?_r=0.

Wood, Michael. "Shangri-La." BBC History. February 17, 2011. http://www.bbc.co.uk/history/ancient/cultures/shangri_la_01.shtml.

Yowangdu Tibetan Culture. http://www.yowangdu.com.

INDEX

INDEX